In the Shadow of the Cross

The Greatest Conspiracy of All Time

In the Shadow of the Cross

The Greatest Conspiracy
of All Time

Billy Roberts

AXIS MUNDI
BOOKS

Winchester, UK
Washington, USA

First published by Axis Mundi Books, 2012
Axis Mundi Books is an imprint of John Hunt Publishing Ltd., Laurel House, Station Approach,
Alresford, Hants, SO24 9JH, UK
office1@o-books.net
www.o-books.com

For distributor details and how to order please visit the 'Ordering' section on our website.

Text copyright: Billy Roberts 2011

ISBN: 978 1 78099 323 2

A CIP catalogue record for this book is available from the British Library.

Design: Stuart Davies

Printed in the USA by Edwards Brothers Malloy

We operate a distinctive and ethical publishing philosophy in all
areas of our business, from our global network of authors to
production and worldwide distribution.

CONTENTS

Introduction   1

Chapter 1. The Birth   7

Chapter 2. The Early Years   17

Chapter 3 The Prophet and the Politician   24

Chapter 4. Jesus Survives the Crucifixion   32

Chapter 5. Scientific and Other Facts   41

Chapter 6. Jesus and Mary Magdelene   50

Chapter 7. Jesus and the Mystery Teachings   58

Chapter 8. The Tomb of Jesus   66

Chapter 9. Miscellaneous — Buddha and Jesus   72

Chapter 10. Discovery of Another Tomb   79

Chapter 11. Esoteric Christianity   83

Chapter 12. The Messianic Line   88

Conclusion   100

Introduction

There are innumerable legends and traditions about the life of Jesus and the work that he did during his sojourn on this planet. Although many of these theories are no doubt based on fact, the majority have been created from pure supposition and conjecture. However, the theory that the life of Jesus did not end on the cross, today appears to have attracted a great deal of interest, and many people do believe this to be more of a fact than a possibility. Although it is only a minority who holds on desperately to the biblical notion that the life of Jesus came to an end on the cross, the evidence to prove otherwise is now beginning to sway even the most fervent supporters of this belief. Over the years, much evidence has come to light, and it would seem that most of the missing pieces about the life of Jesus have in fact been found and the greatest mystery of all time is now that little nearer to being solved.

Although there are many conflicting theories about the life of Jesus, the majority of them do suggest that he survived the crucifixion and, in fact, settled in the East to live on to a ripe old age. In the early years after the crucifixion, a select few possessed knowledge of the secret life of Jesus. This knowledge was carefully handed down through the ages, from one devotee to another, until this very sacred tradition became like a huge chalice of gold. The possessors of this knowledge were eventually driven underground, and in medieval times, a secret organization was formed primarily to protect those who were privy to it, and to prevent them from being branded 'Heretics'. It is believed that such notable people as Leonardo De Vinci and even the great seer Nostradamus, were members of this furtive and extremely elite organization, that many believe was feared by the church.

There is evidence that traditions of a recondite knowledge

have been handed down through the ages; knowledge to which only a very select few could be privy. In fact, one of the early pioneers of theosophy, Annie Besant covered the subject of the Mysteries at some length in her book, *Esoteric Christianity*, in which she explained how the Mystery Schools of ancient Egypt were responsible for keeping the 'occult flame' burning, ensuring its longevity and sacredness.

Before this knowledge could be possessed, the devotees had to prove their worthiness to receive it. As Annie Besant explained, these sacred teachings were very generally known under the term of 'The Mysteries', and were primarily concerned with the deepest facts of man's origin, his nature, and connection with supersensual worlds and beings, as well as of course, with the natural laws of the physical world. Before the student could fully receive the teachings, he was subjected to the most arduous tests and trials, thereby proving that he was spiritually worthy. Once the knowledge was possessed, and initiation had fully taken place, it is believed that the initiate would then be in possession of mystical powers, or Siddhis as they are known in Eastern traditions, thus enabling him to use the hidden forces of nature.

The Mystery Schools produced mystics of the highest kind, and who were able to perform incredible supernatural feats. In fact, looking at initiation into the Mystery Schools from a modern perspective, it would seem the initiates were simply subjected to some sort of 'psychic' development program, in very much the same way that those endeavoring to develop mediumistic skills do today. However, the real Mystery Teachings could not be written down, and in true occult tradition could only be passed on by 'teacher to pupil, mouth to ear'. In fact, the majority of Eastern traditions still possess a deeper core of esoteric teachings that can only be revealed to those who are psychologically and spiritually equipped to receive them. These occult teachings are an integral part of the original scriptures upon which the religion was first founded and were usually only revealed to an aspirant in stages, and even then only when he or she had proved beyond doubt that they were ready. This is the fundamental law underlying the majority of occult teachings, and a 'law' that was more prevalent when Jesus went about his ministry than it is today. In fact, the precept which is still evident today above the portals of the ruins in the so-called 'Mystery' Schools in ancient Egypt, 'MAN KNOW THYSELF' is one that students of the very select and furtive teachings had to prove beyond doubt before initiation could take place. As a member of AMORC, Ancient and Mystical Order of the Rosae Crucis, I fully understand the sensitivity of such teachings and the need for their preservation.

Jesus himself was privy to this *secret knowledge* and had long since been initiated into the very select group responsible for guarding it, which of course they did as though it were gold.

Because the tests and trials to gain entry into the Mystery Schools were so difficult, even the most advanced student very often failed miserably, and as a consequence was rejected. Few achieved attainment, and the weak were forced to abandon their spiritual quest. These either continued their studies in secret until such time that they would be allowed to resume their education in the Mystery Schools, or they immediately prostituted what knowledge they had already gleaned from their teachers, to establish themselves as teachers in their own right.

Once a student of the Mystery Teachings had passed through the various degrees necessary, they would then be initiated into the final level, and thus be allowed to enter the 'Chamber of Divine Knowledge'. Once there, they would be instructed in the deepest and most precious facts pertaining to the evolution of the soul, the universal laws and the nature of Man and the Messengers of God.

With the passage of time, the purveyors of the Mystery Teachings were condemned by the temple priests who saw them as a threat, thus forcing them underground to continue their practices even more furtively. Seeing that the end of the Mystery

Schools was drawing near, and wanting to ensure that the valuable teachings would not be lost forever, the surviving masters meticulously recorded all that they knew, taking great care to transpose the text into a more understandable core of teachings. These teachings were termed 'The Lesser Mysteries' and were and still are today open to interpretation, according the spiritual understanding of the aspirant.

Needless to say, some aspirants had ulterior motives for seeking the spiritual status that accompanied initiation. Once attainment had been successfully achieved, they would use their powers to exploit the weak and the poor and to gratify their own lower passions and desires as well as to amass incredible wealth. However, these too were driven underground and became known as 'The Dark Masters of Evil'. Today their teachings would be propagated and worked by those involved in the black arts and other such abysmal sects.

It is true to say that today the majority of Christians have been indoctrinated into a core of teachings that have been tainted through the ages with the over zealousness of numerous Christian writers, and which now bear no resemblance to the original teachings. In fact, much of what was written about Jesus in the bible was written by later writers either to glorify the entire story, or to perpetuate a myth. Regardless of the reason, the story of Christianity is incredibly beautiful, and the very fact that Jesus has such a huge following today, so long after his death, just proves that he was an incredible human being and a man with charisma and immense power. However, we can never know for certain how much of what we know of Jesus is fact and which of it has been created by Christian writers whose only intention was to glorify a man who many claimed was the earthly incarnation of the Son of God. Nonetheless, we cannot deny that the longevity of the story of Jesus alone is a good indication that he was no ordinary mortal, and as long as we are able to see through the obvious embellishments, the truth will eventually be discovered.

Yoga Ramacharaka suggested in his book *Mystic Christianity*, that once the early Christian Fathers had all passed away, their successors became overzealous in their desire to transform Christianity. As a direct consequence of their efforts to modernize the teachings, the original story was lost completely, and is today buried beneath Church dogma and the misinterpretation of that which is propagated from pulpits by modern-day priests. Christianity no longer bears any resemblance to the way it was in the very beginning, and Christians worldwide still see the cross as a universal symbol and reject any suggestion that Jesus did not die and in fact lived on to a ripe old age. Many false tales were interjected into Christian traditions, and the image the followers have of Jesus today, is in fact far removed from the way he really was. In fact, the story of the Virgin Birth was most likely created in Pagan times, possibly to conceal the fact that Jesus was conceived out of wedlock. Believing wholeheartedly that knowledge of this would defile the name of Jesus, the early Christian writers took pains to create the myth of the Virgin Birth, thus glorifying the name of Jesus to the extent we know it today. However, there is no doubt that Jesus was an incredibly special person, which is probably why such pains were taken to create a beautiful story around his birth and death. Even the story of the Three Wise Men was not fully told. Nor was the part they actually played in the life of Jesus fully revealed. Although today the hierarchy of the Christian Church have half-heartedly admitted that there is a strong chance that Jesus survived the crucifixion and went on to live out his life possibly in Kashmir; it has also been suggested that to accept it publically would shake the very foundations of Christianity, as well as destroy the faith of devout Christians all over the world. This would, in the long term, be detrimental to the whole concept of Christianity, as we know it and would most probably bring about its demise.

Today it would really seem that Christianity is more a

political organization than it is a religion. To hide the truth from the followers of Christianity I am sure you will agree constitutes the greatest conspiracy of all time.

Even as a child I could never quite comprehend the story of the Virgin Birth, nor could I understand why God would allow Jesus to die on a cross, even after he had asked the question, 'Father, why hast thou forsaken me?' The fact that Jesus survived the crucifixion does not take away anything at all from the beautiful story of Christianity, but on the contrary, it makes it even more realistically human by proving once and for all that Jesus was in fact serving a *just* God of compassion, and a God who did hear him when he cried, 'Father, deliver me from this hour'.

Although I have been studying the many different theories about the birth, life and death of Jesus since the mid 1960s, it wasn't until I visited the Rozabal, the alleged tomb of Jesus in Srinagar, Kashmir sometime in 1967, that my eyes were fully opened to the true Christian story. And although my studies have been fairly eclectic, my conclusions now culminate into this book, *In The Shadow Of The Cross — The Greatest Conspiracy of All Time.*

Although my main interest has always been Buddhism, I have had an interest and in fact made a study of all major world religions since the late 1960s. It was never my intention to offend anyone with the contents of this book, but simply to shed even more light on the missing pieces of the life of the greatest man that has ever lived.

Billy Roberts

Chapter One

The Birth

We must remember that Palestine back then was extremely corrupt. Not only did the majority of Jews feel secure under Roman jurisdiction, but the occupying Romans also felt safe knowing that they had the support of the majority of synagogues and the leading Judaic figures. The whole thing was no doubt extremely political. The majority of poor people felt secure in the fact that they had food, water and wine and, as far as they were concerned, the Romans never interfered with the day-to-day running of their trades, and that was all that mattered.

Although the Hebrew communities were extremely close, the rich were strong, and the poor were weak and depended entirely on the wealthy, the moneylenders and the merchants for their survival. The rabbis were very frequently on the Roman payroll, and the wealthy Jewish traders made sure that the Roman governors received their monthly pouches of silver in return for 'special favors'. The synagogues were the focal points of the communities and the rabbis had all the power. The poor Jews awaited some sort of savior — in fact, a Messiah, someone to deliver them from the hell mire in which they were living. Although there were whispers that a Messiah was coming, they were in fact ready to accept anyone who offered a glimmer of hope and freedom. The educated Hebrews never believed it would happen, and even the rabbis and the Jewish fundamentalists had very little faith in the coming of a Messiah.

This dark cloud of despondency gave rise to a spate of charlatans, false prophets and pseudo Messiahs, of which there was no shortage. But then three men who came with traders from Persia stood out from the rest. It was obvious to everyone who saw them that they were of noble blood and very special. They were attired in the robes of kings and spoke with words of wisdom. They were different from the other traders and carried with them no merchandise. They came seeking and not selling. They were very inquisitive and asked many questions about the Hebrew traditions, the workings of the synagogue, the Jewish worship and the temple priests. Deciding not to move on with the other traders, the three men remained in Nazareth.

According to Yogi Ramacharaka in his book *Mystic Christianity*, they sought refuge at a local Inn called 'Barazih'. The Innkeeper was Greek and extremely religious. He had a wife and two daughters and made the three travelers very welcome. Although they were highly thought of by the innkeeper, the three travelers were very cautious of his curiosity, especially about the reason why they were there. They carried with them strange charts depicting the position of the planets in the heavens, and the three men would talk into the early hours of the morning, obviously intent on something quite important. In fact, the three men were leading members of an elite sect known as the Magi, custodians of the world's occult knowledge. They were masters of the highest kind and were faced with the arduous task of keeping the sacred flame of spiritual knowledge burning. They were astrologers and magicians and were obviously in Palestine for a specific reason.

The word *magic* is in fact derived from the word *Magi*, and the word *magician* was originally *magian*, which means one of the Magi. Originally the Magi was the title given to the learned and priestly class of ancient Media and Persia who initially worshipped Ahriman, the god of evil, as well as Ormuzd, the god of good. Zoroaster forbade devil worship, and so the Magi became priests of the reformed faith. They were teachers and philosophers as well as priests. Although the popular belief is that there were in fact three wise men who visited the baby Jesus, the number is not actually mentioned in the biblical narrative. In the Middle Ages, it was claimed that the bones of the Three Wise Men were preserved in Cologne Cathedral and they became celebrated as the Three Kings of Cologne. The names of the three Magi who visited the baby Jesus were said to be Gaspar, Melchior and Balthasar, although religious scholars have questioned this. Gradually in Media and Persia, the Magi were degenerated from the highly respected position they had held, to the rank of jugglers, fortune-tellers and quacks.

Nonetheless, it was understood that the three travelers who came to see the baby Jesus possessed immense supernatural powers, and their presence in Palestine soon gave rise to so much curiosity that they were forced to move from the inn and set up camp just outside of Nazareth. Although the majority of people were just curious about the very dignified visitors to the area, a group of ascetics living in the wilderness, had prophesied that three wise men from the East would one day visit Palestine to pay homage to an extremely special baby boy, destined to wear the Messianic gown. As far as they were concerned, the time had now come. The *Three Wise Men* had arrived.

The Essenes

The news about the three noble travelers quickly reached the Essenic community, a monastic order that had been established on the shores of the Dead Sea for centuries, but with a political rule that extended over a broad area of Palestine. The Essenes were extremely powerful, both spiritually and politically, and they ruled with might and fervor. They were in fact feared by the rabbis and respected by the poor. The Essenes did a lot of good work in the poor community and were known to heal and care for the sick.

Traditionally, Essenes were a peaceful monastic body, but were known locally as 'Spiritual Warriors', who fought for justice and the throne of God. They decried Roman occupation and endeavored to bring the people back to the 'spirit of truth'.

However, the Essenes had known for centuries about the birth of a great Messiah, a chosen one who would deliver the people from the hell mire in which they lived, and bring them back to the true spirit of their original faith. The word was quickly spreading, the long awaited Messiah was most definitely coming and a rush of excitement could be felt all over Palestine. The people of Palestine were tired and were now ready for a Messiah. In fact, for centuries the arrival of a Messiah had been promised, even though the majority of people suspected that this was a promise that had merely been created to give them hope and encouragement, there was nonetheless still a whisper that the time was near and one would soon be born. Believing that their prophesy was about to be fulfilled, a rush of excitement was felt through the Essenic community.

As a greatly respected ancient Hebrew Occult Monastic Brotherhood, the Essenes had been in existence for centuries before the birth of Jesus. They ruled with a strong hand and would not tolerate anybody who exploited the vulnerability of the poorer classes. For this reason, the Essenes kept a watchful eye on the synagogues and were feared by the rabbis. Although primarily a brotherhood of peace, some religious texts suggest that they carried swords and other weapons to protect themselves from their many enemies. The members of the Essenes were extremely disciplined and celibacy was a prerequisite for membership. Before anyone could become a member of this elite sect, they had to meet all the requirements, which involved being subjected to extremely arduous tests and trials. The requirements of the Order were very strict, and its rites and ceremonies of the highest mystical and occult degree. According to various texts, a preliminary apprenticeship of one year was required of the neophyte before he was granted partial recognition as a brother, initially for one year. A further two years had to elapse before he could then be considered as an integral part of the fellowship with the right hand of welcome extended to him.

It would be some years before full membership for the initiate could be granted, and as he was expected to have the knowledge, power and attainment, even then he could not be guaranteed access to the higher circles of the Order. He was expected to be totally dedicated to the Brotherhood, and neither wealth nor influence could secure his position as a fully fledged Essenic Brother. Both neophyte and initiate were expected to abide by all the rules of the Order, which were *obedience*, to give up wealth and all material possessions and demonstrate absolute celibacy. Even the Master of the highest degree had to observe these rules, and anyone breaking them would be immediately expelled from the Order. (*The Order of the Essenes,*Markus Welsby, 1923*)*

No one really expected a Messiah to make an entry into the world by natural means. Even the Judaic intellectuals suspected that the birth would be spectacular and would give them cause to rejoice. Stories changed hands and were exaggerated to the extent that they became something else. Rumors passed quickly from one person to another, and it was decided that the baby King Messiah would be born in humble surroundings, to a young unmarried woman. Although the concept of a Virgin Birth had been spoken of in Judaic circles for centuries, it is uncertain exactly when it became an integral part of Christian teachings. On close scrutiny of the biblical narrative of the Virgin Birth one can see that it was clearly interpolated by later writers, and is only mentioned in Mathew and Luke, albeit very briefly. It is not mentioned anywhere else in the bible and was most definitely not a part of the original teachings. Furthermore, this phenomenon that is an extremely integral part in the wonderful story of Christianity was in fact never referred to at all by any of the disciples of Jesus. In fact, great pains are taken in the bible to give the genealogy of Jesus from David to Joseph, Mary's husband, proving that Jesus was most definitely the son of Joseph and did come from the house of David, in accordance with the Messianic tradition.

Even though the Virgin Birth is only mentioned in the two gospels of Mathew and Luke, Mark and John most certainly make no reference to it at all. It is not even mentioned in the book of Acts, nor is it mentioned in Epistles; even Paul seems to ignore the subject completely and never mentions it at all. In fact, the Virgin Birth does not in any way appear to have been a part of the teachings propagated by the Apostles and really does seem to have been completely unknown to the early Christians. Even though this is clearly the case, on his travels after the crucifixion, Jesus was frequently referred to as 'one who was born of a virgin', a paradoxical title that causes confusion as to the true nature of his birth, and which was most probably the main reason the story of the Virgin Birth was created and interjected later on. Unless such miracles as the Virgin Birth can really happen, then it looks to all intents and purposes that the whole story was created to make Jesus' entry into this world appear more divine and a phenomenon one would expect with the birth of a Messiah. Many religious scholars have suggested that the Virgin Birth was more than likely created much later on, possibly to conceal the fact that Jesus was conceived out of wedlock. This was frowned upon by the Judaic Priests and the hierarchy of the synagogue, and so Mary would have been driven in shame from the village.

And so the whole story of Jesus' entry into this world was by this time already enshrouded in mystery, and the truth about his actual birth will most probably never be known.

Even the story of the Three Wise Men was not fully told, nor was the part they actually played in the life of Jesus revealed.

As previously explained the biblical narration of the birth of Jesus informs us that the Three Wise Men were guided to the birthplace by an unusually bright star in the heavens, and that each of the Magi presented him with a gift of extremely great spiritual significance. Gold, Myrrh and Frankincense were in fact believed to symbolically represent *wealth, pain* and *purity,* and were highly significant where the future life of Jesus was concerned.

Gold was to ensure that Jesus was given a good education, preparing his intellect for the work ahead. *Myrrh* was to constantly remind him of the physical and emotional pains he would have to endure as a King. *Frankincense* was a symbolical representation of purity — the purity of a Messiah and the one who had come to lead his people back to the spirit of truth. Gold, Myrrh and Frankincense are still today considered as symbols of great occult and mystical significance, and even predate the biblical story of Jesus.

It is written in various ancient Islamic texts that the three men came to pay homage to a king, but by the time they had reached Jesus, he was already one year old and living in house and not a stable or a cave as we have been led to believe by the biblical narration. Upon seeing Jesus, the three men simultaneously prostrated themselves in front of him as he sat on Mary's lap, giving him the sacred salutation of a master. It is written that the baby Jesus immediately acknowledged them by outstretching his tiny hand towards them, and pressing his index finger against his thumb, gave them the mystical sign that is used by the Pope today in Papal Benediction, and which in yogic tradition is considered to be the Holy Mudra of a king. This was the confirmation that the Magi needed, Jesus was most definitely the young master who had come to take his place on the great Messianic throne.

The sacred order to which the Magi belonged had in fact known about the birth of Jesus at least 100 years before the actual event took place. They had been informed of the birth through their astrological charts, and with their meticulous mathematical calculations had concluded that there was to be an unusual conjunction of planets in the heavens. Their charts had revealed that the conjunction of Saturn and Jupiter in the constellation of Pisces would eventually be joined by the planet Mars. They knew that the remarkable stellar display produced by all three

planets combined, would in fact have great astrological significance. The extraordinary planetary display not only informed the
Magi of the birth of a great master, but also indicated exactly
where the mystical event was to take place. The constellation of
Pisces influenced the existence of Judea, and considering the
positions of all the other planets in their observations, they were
able to calculate the exact geographical position as well as the
precise time of the birth. Ancient astronomical records in fact
show that not only did all this take place several years before the
traditional date given for the birth of Jesus, but also that he must
have been born sometime in March and not in December as we
have always been led to believe. As these records were kept by
non-Christian bodies, Christians accused them of being
inaccurate and contrived primarily to discredit the whole
Christian story of the birth. In fact, modern astronomical observations have revealed that in the Roman year of 747 — approximately seven years before the traditional Christian birth, such a
conjunction did occur between Saturn and Jupiter in the constellation of Pisces, and that they were joined by the planet Mars in
the early part of 748. Early astronomical texts state that the
notable astronomer Kepler, also made these calculations in 1604,
and modern day astronomers have since verified his conclusions.

However, there is one discrepancy in the Magi's place of
origin. Although it is generally accepted that the three kings
came from Persia, Assyria and Chaldea, some ancient documents
suggest that the coming of a Messiah and the signs of the advent
had only been given to the Israelites, and so the men who were
guided to Jesus by the 'travelling Star' may not have been from
the countries previously mentioned after all, but might well have
been Israelites. Whether or not this is true remains to be seen, and
is such a minor detail that it could not really be detrimental to the
story of the birth of Jesus. There are so many contradictions in the
whole story of Christianity that the onus is on the seeker to
decide which in the biblical narrative is and is not the truth.

So we can see from the events leading up to the birth of Jesus that the Magi had a specific mission and did not come across the baby Jesus by chance. They must have known about his birth for many years and had deemed it a great honor to visit him. However, this was not the last Jesus was to see of the Magi, for it was their intention to return when he was thirteen, at which time his real education would begin. By now, Mary and Joseph fully understood just how special their son actually was and agreed for the three men to return for him. They must have had suspicions from the very moment Jesus was born that he was not like other children and that his time with them was precious.

Even the traditional biblical account of Jesus' life states that as soon as he was able to walk and talk his mother often found him in the temple discussing spiritual matters with the priests. It is said that some of the elders resented the fact that he was much older and wiser than his years and seemed to delight in the frustration and anger he was able to create with his radical views. Other priests admired him and suspected that he was a future prophet and teacher. By the time Jesus had reached the age of thirteen, he was spiritually and intellectually far in advance of other boys his age, and it was clear to his parents it was time for him to leave.

Before leaving with Jesus, it is believed that the three noble travelers met with some of the hierarchy of the synagogues to discuss with them their intentions. This was done more out of politeness than necessity, and it is written that the Magi met with some cynicism from some of the rabbis who dismissed the very suggestion that the young Jesus was 'special' and a Messiah.

Although a minority of church theologians still totally accept the biblical narration of the birth of Jesus as being literally the way it took place, now because so much documented evidence has come to light to prove otherwise, even these diehard church academics are having to re-think the way in which the traditional birth of Jesus is portrayed.

Before we move on with the Magi, we must first go back a little to the period of Jesus' childhood about which very little is known.

Chapter Two

The Early Years

From a very early age, it was clear to all those who knew Jesus that he was a remarkable and most unusual child. From the age of five, he studied the Hebrew law, and even displayed an exceptional talent for mastering both the text and the Hebrew Scriptures. It was said that he would often go missing for hours on end and would be found either in the temple or in the company of passing traders, where he would imbibe their esoteric knowledge and spiritual traditions. Even the biblical account states that they were often amazed with the depth of Jesus' knowledge and understanding, which is believed to have kept them enthralled for hours. And by the time Jesus was eight years old it was clear to everyone in the village of Nazareth that he was no normal child and some proclaimed him even then as a prophet and Messiah.

It was obvious though that the young Jesus did not agree with the traditional Hebrew teachings, and was often antagonistic to the priests and teachers in the temple. Although he won the friendship of many learned men there were also those who opposed and resented him. He was often driven angrily away from the temple, and for a while his parents forbade him to go anywhere near the Hebrew place of worship, for fear of his safety. Jesus was quickly becoming known as a rebel and someone who greatly opposed the Hebrew traditions.

Some Islamic texts suggest that he spent some part of his childhood living with his family in Alexandria in Egypt, then a major centre of learning. Jesus spent a lot of his time in the Great Library there, and was believed to have been able to speak fluent Egyptian. By the time he had reached the age of thirteen, he had long since become a teacher in his own right and had already attracted his own group of loyal followers. Many of those who opposed Jesus could see that he was quickly becoming a threat to Hebrew tradition and that should he be allowed to persist with his rebellious teachings the temple would soon be empty. It was then that the Magi returned to take the young Jesus from his parents. The time had come for the young boy's real education to begin, and this meant visiting many different monasteries and lodges throughout the East.

The Young Jesus Travels

Although an awful lot of what we know about the boy Jesus is no doubt based on supposition and conjecture, a great deal of light has today been shed on the missing years, thus piecing together the greatest mystery of all time. In fact, some interesting facts were brought up in the Mosque Society's book, *The Truth About the Crucifixion*, published in 1978, and which contains a transcript of a seminar attended by speakers from all over the world. The seminar consisted of Christian priests and vicars, religious historians, archaeologists, scientists and experts in Muslim traditions, who together offered their findings to a capacity audience.

The majority of speakers agreed that the three noble travelers were to take Jesus to study in many lands, and would not return until he was a young man and ready to take up his ministry. From then on, the Bible is silent about the young Jesus whose whereabouts appears quite vague. However, this is not the case where various Eastern traditions are concerned, particularly Tibetan, whose monasteries possess documented evidence that the young Jesus sojourned amongst them accompanied by three noble teachers. In fact, it is today fairly common knowledge that Jesus travelled with the Magi to many countries, staying in different monasteries for months at a time where he was educated and instructed in their knowledge and spiritual traditions.

It is thought that whilst the majority of places welcomed the young Jesus, he is believed to have been turned away by a minority who saw him as a troublemaker and rebel. Documented Tibetan and Islamic evidence was produced at the seminar suggesting that the Magi took Jesus to Persia, Egypt, India, Tibet and even China. In Persia even today there is a plateau with an inscription proclaiming that the young Jesus taught there. There is some evidence that the Persian villagers there turned on him for speaking against organized religion and for condemning many of their own beliefs.

In some Tibetan monasteries, there are writings that bear the hallmark of Jesus and legends of a young master who sojourned amongst them, imbibing their teachings and imparting wonderful words of wisdom to the monastic inhabitants. There are also stories handed down through the monastic circles of Tibet suggesting that Jesus was in fact the reincarnation of one of the old prophets, because he exhibited the fire of someone far older than he really was. It is written that the young master's oratory abilities stirred those to whom he spoke, and it was clear that his sole endeavor was no more than to bring them back to the spirit of truth.

While Jesus was looked upon by some as being quite distasteful and a threat to their philosophical and religious beliefs, he was an inspiration to many who praised him as a king and great teacher. Many Eastern esoteric writings state clearly that Jesus travelled with the Magi for seventeen years, preaching and imbibing the knowledge of the countries he visited. This is in fact that part of Jesus' life about which the gospels are completely silent. Some Tibetan and Islamic texts state that Jesus was initiated into the various esoteric schools he visited on his travels, and that he was instructed in the mystic lore and wisdom of the various organizations. In India, Egypt, Persia and other far removed countries he was initiated into the select secret brother-hoods and orders and was revered as a Master. In all these countries, there are stories and legends about the young master who taught there and inspired the people with the wisdom of his teachings. In the remotest areas of the Himalayas and all through Tibet, there are legends about a gifted young orator who spoke marvelous words. His teachings can in fact still be found today recorded in sacred scrolls in temples scattered throughout Tibet and the Himalayas. The Brahmans, Buddhists and Zoroastrians still talk today of a young teacher who once visited their country, inciting the people and causing great opposition amongst the priests. Even at that early age, he was seen to be a religious rebel whose mission and purpose was to cause a religious transformation wherever he visited. Some Tibetan writings state that it was quite clear to all those who met the young Jesus that he was far more than a Jewish prophet. In fact, he was obviously a world spiritual teacher with the spirit of a Messiah. There are ancient traditions and legends throughout Persia of *Issa* the young prophet who taught there in an extremely brave attempt to bring the people back to the spirit of truth. The Hindus tell of a young ascetic called *Jesoph* or *Josa* who travelled to their land accompanied by three wise men, and who opposed the established spiritual laws of their country. Even in China, there are stories of the young spiritual rebel from the East, who taught the poor people of the country instilling in them hope for the future.

The young Jesus made an incredible impact on the places he visited, and the religious scholars he met were also so impressed that they wrote about him in sacred documents. In fact, Jesus made sure that he was remembered, and from the very beginning, he made it quite clear that his primary endeavor was to change the traditional teachings of Judaism and to modernize it. He was against the cliquey atmosphere in the synagogue, and believed strongly that the rabbis always interjected their own personal philosophies into the Hebrew teachings. In fact, there were some who tried to say that Jesus was deranged and had been possessed by demonic forces. However, the young Jesus was far too cunning to allow them to decry him in this way. He was well versed in all religious traditions and always came back with an intelligent and apt retort. In one Tibetan monastery, Jesus was driven away for disagreeing with some of their teachings. However, it is believed that they did allow him to return when he diplomatically apologized and said he was wrong. Once again, the young Jesus was demonstrating wisdom and cunning, simply to be allowed to complete his training in Tibetan wisdom.

Hindu writings say that the years passed slowly by and the child Jesus was fast becoming a young man. The Magi could see that he was nearly ready to begin his ministry and so would soon have to return to Judea. Knowing what an arduous task Jesus had ahead of him, the Magi made quite certain that he was mentally prepared and that he fully understood the seriousness of his future work. Satisfied now that the time had come for Jesus to return to Judea, the noble men who had been constantly by his side for seventeen years finally bade him farewell.

Although outwardly Jesus looked like any other young traveler of the day, inwardly he shone with spiritual enthusiasm as he wended his way home towards Nazareth. His work had truly begun.

When Jesus returned to Judea, he stayed for a short while in various lodges of the Essenes, probably in preparation for the beginning of his work and to conclude his initiation into the Sacred Brotherhood. The biblical narration of the homecoming of Jesus is quite clear, particularly about his meeting with Johannen — John the Baptist and the whole symbolism of Jesus' insistence that John should baptize him and not the other way round. This story clearly indicates that Jesus had been away for some time. John was his cousin and yet Jesus appeared as a stranger to him. John the Baptist was an extremely unusual man and fascinated Jesus. In fact, John was so charismatically powerful that rumors had circulated that he was the Messiah and a reincarnation of one of the old prophets. John the Baptist preached with fire and spirit and heralded the coming of a great master. However, he had no idea whatsoever that the one he awaited was in fact Jesus his own cousin. Their meeting however was of great occult significance and in many ways was an integral part of the final initiation of Jesus into the Sacred Brotherhood of the Essenes. Although the biblical and exoteric account of the actual event is passed over very lightly, it had a much deeper and more profound esoteric significance where the initiation of Jesus was concerned. Those who watched the ceremony are believed to have seen a dove descend from the sky and settle on Jesus' shoulder, and naturally thought that it had been sent directly from heaven. Both Jesus and John then heard a soft voice say, 'This is my beloved son in whom I am well pleased'. This experience had a great and meaningful spiritual significance and is thought to have been the very moment when Jesus became enchristed with a divine power, thus endowing him with the metaphysical abilities he was to use for the rest of his life.

The mystical event is believed to have had psychological implications and disturbed the young Jesus greatly. Although he had been well prepared for the work that lay ahead of him, even at this point Jesus still had no idea who or what he actually was where the Messianic tradition was concerned. Although Jesus was now well educated in the various esoteric traditions, he was still very naive and oblivious to exactly what his life had in store for him.

Although as a young boy he was loved and respected by all the citizens of Nazareth where he lived with his family, when Jesus returned after his travels he was rejected by everyone who probably believed that he had delusions of grandeur, giving rise to the well known biblical precept, 'A prophet is without honor in his own country'. Whether it was this rejection that turned Jesus into the political rebel he actually became, or whether the experience from his travels made him that way, is one thing we will never really know. However, it is certain that Jesus' sole endeavor was to bring the people back to the spirit of truth by inciting them to modernize the old Judaic teachings. Little wonder then why the rabbis grew to resent him, branding him a heretic and political radical. He was obviously an extremely powerful rebel and one thing he desperately wanted was to bring the people back into the synagogue and encourage them not to be led by the rabbis like sheep, but to allow their own voices to be heard.

Chapter Three

The Prophet and the Politician

Although Jesus was a man of peace, there is some evidence in ancient Hebrew and Islamic texts to suggest that both he and his followers carried swords and other weapons to protect themselves against their enemies. Even so, it is not too difficult to see why the figure of Jesus was created in the traditional and exoteric story with which we have become accustomed in the Bible. He was obviously an extremely unusual and charismatic man and someone whose public persona attracted a great deal of interest.

It did not take Jesus very long before he had attracted many followers. Even though he had many devotees, his disciples had to be carefully selected and great care was taken to ensure that they were spiritually and morally suitable to work closely with him. He had been well educated on his travels and possessed a broad knowledge of religion, culture and politics. Even as a child, eager to learn about other religious traditions, he would talk to merchants and other travelers passing through his village, and had always appeared intellectually advanced for his years.

Although his natural dialect was Aramaic, religious scholars have suggested that Jesus was in fact fluent in many different languages. He was obviously now quite refined and in the eyes of many people was a romantic figure. He had in fact become a sort of 'idol' in the eyes of his followers, and fitted perfectly into the archetypal image most people had of a leader. Although initially it was his intention to cause some sort of transformation of Judaic traditions, he was unwittingly used as a political pawn and therefore found himself somehow pulled into a war of politics.

Although the young Jesus did not aspire to be anything more

than a religious teacher, it was his charismatic personality that attracted his innumerable followers, many of whom expected him to do far more than just preach. He never aspired to be anything special, and most certainly never considered himself to be a world prophet outside of the Jewish context. Some of his devotees exploited his abilities and abused his friendship. In fact, it was this that created even more resentment amongst those who opposed him, both in the Jewish hierarchy and in political circles. The politicians of the day were looking for someone with the charisma and oratory skills that Jesus obviously possessed, and the Jews were in great need of a Messiah and someone to lead them from the spiritual mire in which they had found themselves for centuries. As Jesus fitted all the criteria, the synagogue hierarchy were in no doubt that they had at long last found a suitable candidate. The Romans on the other hand were looking for a scapegoat and someone of whom to make an example for the unrest that was stirring amongst the people. Rumors were circulating that Jesus was a troublemaker and an agitator, and some of his supporters began to turn away from him for fear that they too would be branded in the same way. The majority of people were secure under Roman rule and anyone who was a threat to that security was looked upon with some disdain.

Although Jesus still had many followers, his popularity amongst the people was gradually declining. However, he still had his small band of devotees and together they were gradually being driven underground. I suppose it could be said that Jesus was becoming more and more a romantic figure in the eyes of his admirers, amongst whom were whispers that he was the promised Messiah. Being the politician he unwittingly was, Jesus did nothing to discourage this notion. His popularity was obviously quickly spreading and Jesus' name was on everyone's lips, and not always for the right reasons. Joseph of Arimathea was believed to be the only one who truly understood Jesus and was his greatest confidant. Joseph of Arimathea was a wealthy trader of metals, and dealt mainly in tin. This gave rise to suggestions that he had strong links with Britain, and some legends say that Joseph even brought Jesus as a small boy with him on business to Cornwall in England. If this is true then it certainly contradicts the story of the Magi taking Jesus with them to study in various esoteric lodges throughout the East. Unless of course, the Magi also travelled with Joseph and Jesus to England, which I think seems highly unlikely. Incidentally, Arimathea was most certainly not a place. It is a Greek compound word meaning 'Harima Theo' (by the grace of God.) Joseph was also the uncle of Jesus.

To many of the synagogue intellectuals it was clear that Jesus had a specific mission. He was fast becoming a threat to some sectors of the Jewish religious hierarchy who were beginning to view his teachings as the words of a heretic. We must not forget here that the Essenic masters had also been responsible for Jesus' education, and so had a vested interest in him. They were beginning to disapprove of some of the things he did and issued him with warnings that they did not condone what he was doing. You might say that Jesus was looked upon as a very 'loose cannon' by some of the Essenic Brethren, who really wanted to disown him. However, the majority of Essenes still had great faith in him and supported him whole-heartedly in the hope that he would eventually achieve everything they expected of him.

The figure the people saw preaching was no ordinary man, but someone with a highly developed mind and powers that had been carefully and meticulously cultivated over the seventeen years he had been travelling. In fact, it is not difficult to see exactly why Jesus was able to hold the attention of those to whom he preached. His carefully designed sermons enthralled young and old alike, and even the intellectuals began to see profound wisdom in his words.

Jesus knew that his enemies were growing in number and that

he would not be allowed to continue preaching for very much longer. Although he still had many loyal followers, there were only twelve who were actually privy to the deeper teachings into which he himself had been initiated when he was a young boy. Jesus called his closest disciples to the room above the inn, known to his initiates as *'The Kingdom'*. It was in fact here that Jesus passed on his most sacred teachings to his disciples, with the sole intention of preparing them so that they could continue his work after he had gone. Jesus knew full well that this was to be the *Last Supper,* the symbolism of which would echo forever through time. There is no doubt that even before that memorable night Jesus was only too aware of his fate and knew exactly who it was that would betray him.

The biblical account of the Last Supper has somehow left a profound mark upon Christianity as we know it today, although in reality its spiritual implications were in fact much deeper. Jesus always instructed his disciples over a meal, which they always ate together in the sacred chamber above the inn. Judas was in fact a co-operator in the greatest conspiracy of all time and was used by the Romans as a pawn primarily to bring down the political hold Jesus had on many of his followers. Although it was the intention of Judas to betray Jesus, the thirty pieces of silver he actually received for the betrayal were incidental. It might be said that Judas was in fact a double spy, for scholars have suggested that both the Romans and the followers of Jesus had carefully contrived the whole scenario of the betrayal. Judas was loyal to Jesus and simply played along with those who sought his destruction, just as he had been instructed. However, the plan went drastically wrong and the call for the demise of Jesus looked like the end of his reign. Judas saw this as failure and thought that he had badly let Jesus down. Unable to live with this thought, and thinking that he had also betrayed his fellow disciples, Judas hanged himself.

The suicide of Judas immediately unnerved the other

disciples. They became suspicious of each other and also began to doubt that Jesus was exactly who they had previously thought. The disciples' doubt quickly spread into fear and they went underground, denying Jesus and each other whenever necessary to save their own lives.

After the arrest of Jesus, the doubt the disciples had in the man they had followed deepened even more. They wondered whether he really was the Messiah and the chosen one after all. Their faith in Jesus had been put to the test and they failed miserably. The group quickly disbanded and went into hiding for fear of losing their own lives. From this point on the biblical account of the story is quite clear and yet relies primarily upon faith. The account affirms that Jesus was crucified and rose from the dead — but what happened then? Luke was a physician and scholars have suggested that he managed to administer a herbal narcotic to Jesus whilst he was on the cross. This would have induced a catatonic state, ensuring he did not feel any pain and that to all intents and purposes he appeared dead. Furthermore, it is known that Jesus was not left on the cross for the customary period to die a slow agonizing death as was the usual custom. Believed to be dead he was taken down after only three hours and delivered into the hands of Joseph of Arimathea. From then on the biblical narration of the event is somewhat distorted and relies a great deal on faith and belief. The fact that Jesus was removed prematurely from the cross may well have been due to the fact that he was crucified on Friday, and the following day being Sabbath and such an important sacred day, meant that it was forbidden for anyone to remain nailed to a cross. That part of the story was most probably just a coincidence and had nothing to do with Pilate's intervention or the fact that he was Jesus, the Messiah and Savior, as millions of Christians still believe today.

The Bible states that Paul saw Jesus on the road to Damascus in AD 35, after the crucifixion. In fact, it was Paul's intention to bring Jesus back for a second crucifixion. St Ignatius wrote to the

Smyrneans about AD 70, suggesting that they 'both knew and believed' that Jesus had not died on the cross and was in fact still very much alive. In fact, rumors began to circulate that Jesus was still alive and that he had made a miraculous recovery after his death. Jesus had already proved to his admirers that he was a most unusual man and someone who possessed supernatural skills. Therefore, it was quite easy to believe that he had been rescued from the cross by some Divine power, thus proving once and for all that he was the long awaited Messiah. And so, in the tradition of Chinese whispers so the story of the resurrection grew, and kept on growing to the way it is told today.

Before the cross became a symbol of Christianity, a fish was used as a symbol of recognition. As it was not always wise to draw this or scratch it in the sand or on the wall, this was converted into crossed fingers. Today we cross our fingers for luck or to ensure that we are protected when telling an untruth; however, crossed fingers were originally a secret symbol of Christian faith, and were used by the followers of Jesus to identify themselves to other devotees.

We must not lose sight of the fact that Jesus was to all intents and purposes no ordinary man. Regardless of whether or not you believe that he was the chosen Messiah, there is still far too much evidence for us to dismiss the information that he most certainly was a man of immense intelligence and did possess extraordinary metaphysical powers. This being the case he could quite easily have avoided crucifixion, or even used his powers in some way to prove to his persecutors that he was who his followers thought he was. All the evidence points to the fact that this is not what Jesus wanted, and it was vitally important to the entire Messianic plan that he saw it through to the very end. It is quite clear from secret documents that have been discovered that Jesus never thought of himself as a Messiah or Chosen One, and in fact it was not until much later that he really realized that he was much more than a spiritual teacher and healer. The weight of this realization is believed to have had a profound effect upon him and troubled him so much that he spent many days in meditation and prayer.

One other theory that has been suggested is that it was not Jesus who was crucified but his twin brother, Thomas. However, this theory is more speculation rather than fact and merely suffices to complicate the story of Jesus even more, and is definitely a theory that really does not stand up against all the other evidence.

There have also been suggestions that being crucified was not an actual part of Jesus' plan, and that this only happened when he was about to leave Palestine to begin his search for ten of the twelve tribes of Israel. Jesus was a strategist but it did seem at this point that his carefully thought out plan to raise his profile as a public spiritual figure before he went on his travels had gone drastically wrong. Some religious scholars have suggested that Jesus most probably conspired with Judas to create the plan for the betrayal and ultimate arrest, and although Mary Magdalene, Nicodemus and Joseph of Arimathea were said to have been privy to the well-kept secret, the rest of the disciples were completely unaware of it. What is certain is that at this point in Jesus' ministry the rabbis wanted to discredit him by proving that he was not the long awaited Messiah as everyone had thought. An ideal way of doing this was to make certain that he suffered death by crucifixion, thus showing his followers that he was mortal and not divine and that God had allowed him to die. Once this had been achieved it was hoped that his many followers would lose heart and return to worship in the synagogue.

We must however bear in mind that like other stories of the life of Jesus that do not have the documented evidence to support them, they can only be regarded as theories. Nonetheless, it is still very difficult to ignore some of the evidence that is now coming to light about the missing years of Jesus and the life he eventually lived in Srinagar, Kashmir many years after the crucifixion. As I have already stated in a previous chapter The Mosque Society in London published two very interesting works, *The Truth About the Crucifixion,* consisting of transcripts from an international conference on the Deliverance of Jesus from the Cross, attended by representatives from many religions. Each attendee presented evidence to support their individual beliefs that Jesus not only survived crucifixion, but then went on to live to a ripe old age. The second book is *Jesus in India: An Account of Jesus' Escape from Death on the Cross and his Journey to India.* This was written by Hazrat Mirza Ghulam Ahmad of Qadian, the founder of the Ahmadiyya Movement in Islam, and presented some extremely fascinating evidence about Jesus' survival. Even the Holy Quran affirms that Jesus was born without a father and did not die an accursed death on the cross, a belief that is firmly held by the majority of Eastern religions.

According to the biblical accounts of Jesus' ministry, he only preached for a couple of years in Palestine in comparison with the rest of his work in many other countries, and yet today there are over 800 million Christians all over the world, which I'm sure you will agree says it all.

Although many theories have been put forward over the years, and no end of books written about the life of Jesus beyond the cross, the story of Jesus living to a ripe old age in Srinagar, Kashmir, is one that has been fairly consistent throughout this very controversial subject.

Chapter Four

Jesus Survives the Crucifixion

If Jesus really did survive death on the cross, what could have happened to him after he recovered from his horrific ordeal? Some schools of thought believe that once his persecutors discovered that he was still alive, Jesus knew that it was not safe for him to remain in Palestine. He was still very weak and it was obvious that he would not have survived crucifixion a second time. Jesus knew that there would be a ransom on his head and so heeding his friends' warnings he went into hiding until his wounds had completely healed and his strength had fully returned. Jesus' biggest fear was that he would be caught and crucified again, and he knew that if that happened his persecutors would make sure this time that he was really dead. He was suspicious of most people and trusted only a very small handful of those he regarded as close friends. Apart from his mother, Mary Magdalene was his closest friend and someone he admired and trusted.

The first to meet Jesus after he had recovered was in fact Mary Magdalene and her companion. The biblical account of the meeting states that she kissed his feet, the first indication that Jesus stood physically before her and not as a spirit. The Bible goes on to say that Jesus instructed Mary Magdalene to tell his disciples to go to Galilee where he would meet them. Jesus was then met by James and Paul, and he made contact with other friends at various meeting places. Jesus could not risk being recognized and so had to take great care not to be seen. This account of the story shows that Mary Magdalene was overjoyed to see that Jesus was still alive, and was afraid for his safety. This is not something one would expect had Jesus been a spirit and not a tangible flesh and blood body. Jesus himself was aware of the dangers and tried to comfort her. In an effort to throw his persecutors off his track, Jesus then travelled about 100 kilometers towards Galilee. Here there was more evidence that Jesus was still alive in a physical body when he met his apostles. In the Gospel of St Luke we can read in Chapter 24, verses 37–39: 'But they were terrified and affrighted, and supposed that they had seen a spirit. And he said unto them: Why are ye troubled? And why do thoughts arise in your hearts? Behold my hands and feet that it is I myself; handle me and see; for a spirit hath not flesh and bones as ye see me have'.

A further two verses on Jesus clearly shows signs that he is hungry, not something one would expect from a spirit. His disciples cooked him broiled fish and watched as he ate it with honeycomb. (Luke 24: 41–43.)

In the Gospel of St John, it says that Thomas touched Jesus' wounds, again proving that he was alive in a physical body and not standing before his disciples in spirit.

If the biblical account of the story is true and Jesus did die on the cross at the age of 33, what about the statements he made in which he said, 'And I have other sheep that are not of this fold: I must bring them also, and they will heed my voice. So there shall be one flock, one shepherd' (John 10: 16–17) and 'I am sent only to the lost sheep of the House of Israel' Mathew, 10: 5–6)?

Through all the statements that Jesus made, it was in fact quite obvious that his mission was specific, and that was to reunite the remaining ten of the twelve lost tribes of Israel who had been scattered in different countries.

And so after educating his disciples in the secret teachings for a further 18 months, Jesus fled Palestine for fear that he would be recaptured. News had broken that he was still alive and those who had loyally supported him were eager to find him. Besides, his mission of finding the lost tribes of Israel had not yet been fulfilled, and so accompanied by Mary Magdalene, his mother

Mary, Thomas (allegedly the twin brother of Jesus known as Ba'bad), and a few other devoted followers, Jesus left Palestine and began his arduous journey towards the east. By now the rumor that Jesus was still alive had begun to quickly spread all over Palestine, thus rekindling the story of the Messiah. Even then Jesus was still extremely weak both physically and mentally and could not afford to be caught and crucified a second time. And so to avoid being recognized he travelled incognito under the name of Yuz Asaph. The name Yuz is taken from the Hebrew word, Yusu which means 'Jesus', and Asaph means 'The Gatherer'. In fact, in Jesus' case, one who was to gather the ten lost tribes of Israel. This was to be the life mission of Jesus and the sole purpose of his existence in accordance with the Messianic tradition. Another interpretation of the name Asaph is 'leader of those he cured of leprosy'.

Jesus' Mother Dies

Jesus and his small entourage attracted large crowds wherever they went. The Majority of those who listened to his teachings were enthralled by his wisdom and wanted to become one of his followers. However, in many of the other places Jesus and his group visited they were met with hostility. In fact, many people branded him a 'false prophet' and even accused him of being a heretic, and forced him to move on. The years soon passed by and Jesus' Mother was becoming very weary. There is no biblical account of Mary's death and the apostles are silent about it. Considering she played such an important part in the life of Jesus, not an awful lot is said of her after the resurrection. However, many of the writings in some Eastern literature are quite clear about exactly what happened to her. Sadly, the journey proved to be too difficult for Mary, and she died in a place that is known today as Murree, on the border of Pakistan. Murree is situated about forty miles from Taxila and approximately thirty from Rawalpindi. In fact, until 1875, Murree was called Mari and was named after her. Mary is buried on a hilltop known as Pindit-Point where her tomb can be found today. Mary's tomb is attached to the Defense Tower and is called *Mai Mari Da Asthan,* meaning 'The resting place of Mother Mary'. Her tomb faces east-west, in accordance with Judaic tradition, rather than north-south as in Islamic custom. This is a clear indication that Mary had in fact traversed with her son, Jesus, over the beautiful high terrain of Afghanistan and Pakistan, confirming the verse in the Quran: 'And We made the son of Marium (Mary) and his mother a sign, and gave them refuge on an elevated land of green valleys and springs of running water' (Al-Mu'minun 23:51).

Mary's sepulcher had in fact fallen into disrepair, and in 1950 was extensively restored. Although the tomb is situated in a very precarious military location, pilgrims still visit it every day, primarily to pay homage to a very special mother — the mother of Jesus.

Jesus' entry into Kashmir can be historically traced through a valley called Yusu Margh, which is almost certainly named after him. It is in this valley that the race of Yadu Jews can be found even today. It seems to be quite clear that Jesus knew exactly where he was going to settle, and although the lost tribes of Israel were scattered in many countries, Kashmir held some special spiritual significance for Jesus, of that much religious scholars are certain. However, before Jesus and his small group of followers had reached Kashmir, they had visited Afghanistan and many other countries throughout the East, retracing his childhood steps. Today in a Tibetan monastery there can still be found parchments containing writings which bear the hallmark of the teachings of Jesus, especially the parable of *The Sower,* and which leave no doubt in the minds of some religious scholars that Jesus visited there before and after the crucifixion.

Although the biblical account of the events after the crucifixion appears somewhat vague, Jesus' actual passage into

Kashmir is clearly documented in ancient writings found in various monasteries in Tibet and Indian. Jesus is believed to have been 60 years old when he actually entered Kashmir, and judging by the warm welcome he received it was clear that news that he was coming had already reached the people there.

As I have mentioned previously it is also believed that after the crucifixion Jesus remained with his disciples for a year and a half before leaving for the East. In the Gospel of St Thomas, we can read that the disciples said to Jesus, 'We know that you are going to leave us. Who shall then be chief over us?' Jesus said to them, 'Wherever you have come, you shall go to James, the righteous one' (Bertil Gartner: *The Theology of the Gospel According to Thomas*, p.56–57) and 'But the days shall come when you shall seek me and you shall not find me'(*The Gospel of St Thomas Logian*, 38).

The above passages offer even more confirmation that Jesus had not died on the cross. He in fact remained with his disciples to prepare them for the work that he wanted them to continue when it was time for him to leave. Besides everything else, Jesus needed to ensure that his disciples fully understood the depth of the teachings they had to pass on, as well as to conclude the final part of their initiation. He especially prepared Peter and James to look after his sheep in his absence, but actually nominated James to take his place as the disciples' leader.

A parchment containing 30 pages of further information about the events after the crucifixion was found on the border between Egypt and Sudan. The parchment informs us that Jesus was alive after the crucifixion and was actually seen in the flesh, assuring his followers that he was very much alive and with them.

The Dead Sea Scrolls that were found in caves in the valley of Qumran by a shepherd boy in 1947 also shed some light on the missing years of Jesus. These scrolls speak repeatedly of the *Teacher of Righteousness*, probably the same teacher mentioned in the Book of Damascus. Parchments throwing even more light on the life of Jesus were discovered in Nag Hammadi, a village in Egypt. These were written in the Coptic language, and were believed to have been hidden from the early Roman Church whose members were intent on destroying such literature. The find consisted of 52 writings, 1,191 pages in total, and were thought to be the literature of the Gnostics the Hebrew Christians and the more pious of the early Christian Community.

The writings had been buried underground in a graveyard by early Christians, and contained the Gospel of St Thomas, with the early version of 114 precepts of Jesus, many of which cannot be found today in the synoptic Gospels. The writings contain some very significant dialogues that Jesus had after the crucifixion. The discovery also included the Gospel of St Philip, the Gospel of Truth and the Epistle of James. The discovery was without a doubt a huge revelation and highlighted some very important points in the history of Christianity. From the discovery of these documents, it is quite clear that the death of Jesus on the cross was a myth created by some very frightened early Christians who simply wanted to perpetuate the traditional story of the death of Jesus. Hebrew hymns following a similar theme were also discovered at the same time, and were attributed to the same teacher. In fact, many Hebrew writings up to the first century AD also came to light. At that particular time, the Jews were divided into three sects, the Pharisees, the Sadducees and the Essenes. Jesus and John the Baptist grew up among the Essenes, also making the writings much more credible.

Secret Document and the Freemasons

An ancient document known as the Essenian Epistle was discovered in a monastery at Alexandria in the late nineteenth century. This incredible find, written in Latin, was translated into German before falling into the hands of the Freemason Society, whose strict code of secrecy regarding all such ancient documents meant the contents could not be revealed. However, the German translation of the epistle had already been copied and was then translated into English. In 1975 though, the Freemason Society was compelled to reveal the fact that they possessed the German translation of the epistle, and as a result, a limited amount was printed for general circulation. According to informed sources, the epistle throws a great deal of light on the events of Jesus' life after the crucifixion.

In fact, it is said to be clear from the contents of the epistle that the early Christian Fathers were in full possession of the truth about the life of Jesus, and knew that he survived the crucifixion to live on to a ripe old age. The story though was totally distorted by the early Christian Fathers, who changed it to the version with which we are more or less familiar today. For one thing, they originally said that Jesus was crucified between the ages of 40 to 45 and not 33, as is the traditional belief. The epistle is also reputed as saying that there was nothing unusual about Jesus being accompanied by Thomas on his visit to India, as Jesus accompanied the preachers of the gospels everywhere. In fact, regardless of how ridiculously clumsy the early Christian Fathers' efforts were to cover up the true accounts of the life of Jesus, particularly after the crucifixion, it is blatantly obvious that this was done to preserve the myth that they had created about his birth and death. Such a seal of secrecy, as created by the early Christian church, made it all the easier for the ordinary person to follow the traditional doctrine of the church, particularly as they saw to it that only one existed.

All the Apocryphal and Gnostic literature describes the events after the crucifixion of Jesus, and also highlight the plans Jesus had for his disciples' missionary campaign. He nominated Thomas as missionary to India, and as a result, he went to stay in Taxila and is believed to have been so successful there that he succeeded in converting King Gondophorus to Christianity.

From then on, the life of Jesus can be more or less reconstructed by collating the information from different sources. However, there are contradictions regarding the period in which Jesus visited some countries. For an example, from various writings it is known that Jesus visited the Himalayas. However, whether he visited the Himalayas before the crucifixion or after is a little vague. The ancient Hindu scriptures called the Puranas presents a clear indication that he did visit the Himalayas when he responded to an inquiry by the king. Jesus told him that he was the 'Messiah that arose in a foreign land.' The Puranas, an encyclopedia of Hindu religious literature, state quite positively that the way in which Jesus responded to the king left very little doubt that the event took place after the crucifixion and not before. It is not quite clear though who the king was exactly. In the Puranas, the king Jesus met is referred to as Salivahana, and according to certain sources, and more specifically the Encyclopedia Americana, 1976 Edition headed 'India — Post Asoka India', traditionally, Salivahana came to power in the second century and was named Gautami Putra Satakarni. This would mean then that when Jesus actually met the king he would have been just over 100 years old.

Over the years, there has been a lot of speculation about the teachings that Jesus propagated both before and after the crucifixion. There are strong similarities between his teachings and the teachings of Buddha, leading scholars to conclude that Jesus had studied Buddhism and in fact converted to Buddhism. The more skeptical of those studying the life of Jesus say that he plagiarized Buddha's teachings and frequently used Buddhist precepts in his discourses. Nineteenth-century writer and traveler, Nicolas Notovitch, whilst on a visit to a Tibetan Monastery, was allowed to see some ancient manuscripts containing writings ascribed to Jesus. Although Buddhist in style, the text apparently contained precepts similar to those expounded by Jesus in the biblical accounts of his sermons. If Jesus had really been responsible for the ancient text then he had been greatly influenced by the teachings of Buddha. If the ancient Tibetan manuscripts really contained the genuine teachings of Jesus, then it is quite obvious that he studied Sanskrit Pali and had read the Vedas and Buddhist Canon. Many of the ancient writings held in the Tibetan Monasteries had seemingly come directly from the mouths of Jewish merchants who passed through the country directly after the crucifixion. There is also some evidence to suggest that Jesus himself did stay in some of the Tibetan Monasteries, imbibing their teachings and imparting his wisdom to the Tibetan Masters. The writings were mostly written in Pali, the sacred language of Southern Buddhism, although some were apparently written in Aramaic the language of Jesus.

Jesus' presence in Srinagar attracted the interest of King Gopananda (the name varies in different accounts of the story) who was building numerous temples through Kashmir. Upon the invitation of the king, an expert mason by the name of Sulaiman came from Persia to conduct repairs to the throne of Solomon on the top of a hill. Objections were raised by the Hindus who complained that Sulaiman was not of their faith and had come from a foreign country and so could not therefore work on the restoration. King Gopananda sent word to Yuz Asaph (Jesus) saying, 'if you are who you say you are restore order so that work can continue'. Yuz Asaph is reported to have done what the king asked of him, and in return, his name was added to one of the pillars along with the masons who carried out the work under the supervision of Sulaiman. According to records, the inscriptions on the pillars read: *Bhisti Zargar, year 54, Khawaja Rukun, the son of Mirjan; Yuz Asaph proclaimed his prophethood: year 54. Yusu, of the tribes of Israel.* Although the inscription is now worn with time, Yuz Asaph's name is there to be seen, more evidence that he survived the crucifixion to live on in Kashmir to a very old age. Furthermore, today the people of Kashmir still revere Yuz Asaph as an exalted being and still talk about him with great respect.

Chapter Five

Scientific and Other Facts

If Jesus had survived his crucifixion, how did this really happen?

As far as we are told, Jesus was born around 9 BC and was crucified sometime between AD 30 and AD 33 and was taken from the cross and placed in a tomb that was owned by his alleged uncle, Joseph of Arimathea. It is quite important to note that this tomb was not filled with earth, as was the Judaic custom, but was only secured by a large stone. In the tomb, Jesus was tended by Nicodemus who applied ointment, which helped to heal the wounds and improve the circulation. This ointment can still be found on sale in Palestinian apothecaries today and is called either *Marham-I-Isa*, meaning the ointment of Jesus, or *Marham-I-Rasul*, meaning the ointment of the prophet. In fact, the ointment is mentioned in many Eastern medical journals, which state that it was the ointment applied to the wounds of Jesus when he was taken down from the cross. There would have been no point applying ointment to the wounds of a dead man in the tomb. Jesus was obviously still very much alive when delivered from the cross but probably in a deep comatose state. Furthermore, the tomb was not a small chamber but was spacious enough to accommodate Mary Magdalene, his mother Mary and Salome when they visited him. The very fact that the stone had been moved from the entrance of the sepulchre is perhaps an indication that Jesus had left it physically and not in a supernatural way as the biblical story suggests.

It is also important to take a look at the events leading up to the crucifixion to see that there is every reason why Jesus did not die on the cross. For example, Pilate displayed a great deal of sympathy towards Jesus and allowed his body to be delivered to friends and not his enemies. In addition, Jesus was not left the customary period on the cross but was taken down after only a few hours. It was not the purpose of crucifixion to cause immediate death, but was inflicted as a torture. The legs were frequently broken to accelerate death, and then the body usually left hanging for days until vultures or other wild predators had devoured it. Jesus was not subjected to this hideous and horrific torture, as were others who were crucified. Furthermore, although a spear pierced his side, his legs were not broken, as was the usual practice with crucifixion. It is further believed that to prevent Jesus being arrested a second time, Joseph of Arimathea conspired with Nicodemus to perpetuate the story of Jesus dying on the cross. Many of the followers of Jesus desperately tried in vain to find his tomb. This is one of the primary reasons that rumors quickly circulated that Jesus had in fact died and ascended to heaven.

Although a minority of scientists have stated that in their opinion the so-called Shroud of Turin is not the actual burial cloth of Jesus, the extensive research performed on the Shroud has caused others to conclude that it is the actual cloth in which Jesus was wrapped after the crucifixion. However, before we can draw any conclusions about the scientific findings we must first take a look at the evidence.

In 1969, a Swiss professor specializing primarily in criminology, made a detailed scientific analysis of the Shroud of Turin, subjecting it to a process called palynology. This in fact is the study of plant pollen that can be found in cloth. Using every available scientific method, it took Professor Max Frei of Zurich two years to perform his meticulous analysis of the cloth. Through the process he used he discovered a minute layer of a dust of unknown origin. A further analysis revealed that the dust was in fact composed of minute grains of fossilized pollen of plants, which existed in Palestine 2000 years ago. Professor Frei was convinced that the Shroud was genuine and was prepared to put his reputation as a worldwide criminologist on the line. His word made the whole scientific process much more credible. For not only was Professor Max Frei a worldwide criminologist, but he was also director of the Zurich Police Scientific Laboratory and possessed a degree in biology and natural sciences.

First of all, Professor Frei used microscopic analysis to examine the pollen. After this, he put the particles through the process known as palynology to determine the pollens' structure and geographical and paleobotanical distribution in the form of microfossils, comparatively. This process led him to then conclude that the plant originated in the Palestine area. Max Frei also discovered that there were fragments of plants from the Constantinople area, where the Shroud had been exhibited from the year 438 onwards. Max Frei also discovered samples of dusts from the Mediterranean from around the fourteenth and fifteenth centuries. Pollen from six plants from Palestine was in fact found, one from Constantinople and eight from the Mediterranean area.

The investigations continued for seven years, after which some of the scientists concluded that Jesus had been buried alive. Although not all the scientists agreed to the Shroud's authenticity, it was agreed that whoever was wrapped in it most certainly did not die on the cross. Twenty-eight bloodstains found on the Shroud supported this theory, as the body would not have bled in the same way as whoever *was* wrapped in the cloth. Although it cannot be proved that it was definitely the Shroud in which Jesus was wrapped, it is a little more than coincidental that whoever was wrapped in it had suffered exactly the same punishment we are told Jesus himself suffered, even down to the crown of thorns.

In more recent tests carried out on the Shroud, it was disclosed that although there were innumerable people executed in that way, the linen cloth was in fact the one in which the body of Jesus had been wrapped. Crucifixion was quite common as a method of punishment at that time, but the way in which the punishment of Jesus was administered was somewhat different from all the others.

A computer used to analyze photographs sent from Mars by the Viking probes was used in a final attempt to either confirm the Shroud's authenticity or prove once and for all that it was a fake. The computerized analysis of an ultra-violet photograph that had been taken of the Shroud in 1969 by Giovan Battista Judica Cordiglia, reconstructed the weft of the cloth, showing it to be identical to linen used at the time of Jesus' crucifixion.

The presence of organic substances in the linen revealed by this computerized process also helped to confirm the Shroud's authenticity or at least the period from which it originated. Blood, sweat, saliva, fossilized pollen, aloes, and myrrh of around eleven different species were found, six of which were from plants now extinct, but which most definitely existed in Palestine 2,000 years ago. The group of American scientists were now more or less convinced that this was the burial Shroud of Jesus. The marks left by the crown of thorns, the semi-coagulated blood on the middle thorax, which flowed from the wound inflicted by the spear, the numerous wounds caused by scourging and the holes made by the nails in the wrists and feet, collectively confirmed their conclusions that it was genuine and not a fabrication from the Middle Ages. Apart from the fact that the image on the linen revealed that the legs had not been broken, as was the tradition with crucifixion, further conclusions were drawn from the overall image of whoever had been wrapped in the Shroud. The scientific analysis showed that the discernible images on the Turin Shroud had not been made by the body's contact with the cloth, but by an unusual outpouring of energy from the body itself, which the American scientists could not explain. Not only was the person who was wrapped in the cloth still very much alive, but he must have possessed some sort of metaphysical power for there to have been such a release of energy from his body. Although this phenomenon cannot be explained we can only conclude that if the Turin Shroud is genuine, then it must be the actual burial cloth of Jesus.

A more detailed analysis of the Shroud revealed that there had been a coin placed over each eye. A closer inspection showed that the dates on the coins corresponded to the exact time of the calculated crucifixion of Jesus. It was also discovered that the actual Shroud itself was most probably some sort of tablecloth, possibly the one used at the historical Last Supper. Even with these facts, many of those who researched the Turin Shroud remained skeptical and still refused to accept that it was genuine. This could have been a proverbial 'cover-up' by the Church of Rome, which would really prefer to perpetuate the biblical narrative of Jesus dying on the cross, and not surviving his crucifixion to live on to continue his good work in the East.

Not all those making a detailed analysis of the Shroud were convinced of its authenticity. Although the church was not in favor of the research, they did reluctantly give permission for the scientific analysis to be carried out. One of the first detailed analyses performed on the Shroud concluded that the weave was in fact a medieval fake, and that the herringbone weave was definitely not 2,000 years old. It wasn't until a non-scientific husband and wife team made a startling suggestion that more tests were carried out. It was discovered that the Shroud had at some point in time been repaired, and that a more recent weave had been meticulously woven in to the original cloth. In the original analysis a portion of the Shroud had been selected at random, and that piece of cloth had in fact been used to repair the Shroud in medieval times. Had this not been suggested by the non-scientific couple, the Shroud may have been disregarded as one of many religious fakes and most probably lost forever.

A bloodstained cloth now known as the Sudarium of Oviedo, measuring approximately 84 x 53 cm and thought to be the cloth that was wrapped around the head of Jesus after the crucifixion, is kept in the Cámara Santa of the Cathedral of San Salvador, Oviedo, Spain. The Sudarium (Latin for 'sweat cloth') now quite fragile, is stained with sweat and blood that match those on the Shroud of Turin. In 1998, blood tests done on both the Sudarium and the Shroud of Turin confirmed that the bloodstains on both cloths were of the same type, AB, a blood type common among Middle Eastern people but fairly rare among medieval Europeans. On close examination the material of both the Shroud and the Sudarium were found to be the same but with obvious differences in the manner of weaving. Even with all this evidence experts are still loath to say the cloth is genuine.

Further revelations came to light in the form of books discovered buried beneath an ancient synagogue in Cairo. The books contained at least two hundred thousand pages of ancient Hebrew script, recounting the story of a 'Teacher of Righteousness'. The discovery, known as the Zadokite document, was of great spiritual significance, and appeared to throw a lot of light on the life of Jesus after the crucifixion, telling how he fled from Jerusalem to Damascus. Although Jesus was not actually named in the books, religious scholars are in no doubt that the 'Teacher of Righteousness' mentioned in the ancient documents is a direct reference to Jesus. Fragments of the ancient documents, dating from the first-century AD, were also discovered in the Valley of Qumran in the *Dead Sea Scrolls*, mentioned previously.

If Jesus did survive the crucifixion, as so many people now believe, the whole story of Christianity would have to be re-written. This would have an incredible impact on Christianity as a whole, and would force the Christian Church to re-think its religion. A lot would be at stake, and this would mean the end of Christianity as we know it today.

Other Pieces of Interesting Scientific Evidence

One other theory about the image on the Shroud of Turin was put forward by Paul Vignon, who suggested that it had been produced by ammoniacal vapors reacting to the aloe-impreg-nated cloth. Professor Hirt, however, suggested that in his opinion the marks on the shroud could only have been caused by flowing blood. Coagulated blood on the flesh would not leave a stain and neither would a corpse actually bleed.

During the extensive excavation of a burial area in June 1968, Israeli builders unearthed three burial tombs containing human remains. Curiosity was aroused when one of the workmen discovered an inscription outside one of the burial chambers stating: *Jehohanan who met his death by crucifixion.* Dr Nicu Haas of the Department of Anatomy, Hebrew University-Hadassah Medical School, made a closer and more detailed inspection of the remains, and found evidence to suggest that whoever it was in the tomb had most certainly suffered the most horrific death through crucifixion. A carefully detailed analysis of the remains revealed that a nail had been driven through the bones of the forearm, a clear indication that the victim would have been in excruciating agony before dying. The lower bones on both legs (the tibiae and the fibula) had been severely fractured, most probably the result of a forceful blow that rapidly caused the victim's demise. The victim's feet were also joined together with the insertion of a single nail, giving a similar anatomical appearance to the image on the Turin Shroud, with one signif-icant difference — Jesus' legs were not broken.

Another Burial Cloth

A burial cloth similar to the Turin Shroud was discovered during an excavation at Antinoe, a small town that had been built on the River Nile in Egypt around AD 132, by the Roman Emperor, Hadrian. The discovery was made by Albert Gayert between 1897–1902 who at the time believed he had unearthed a piece of significant archaeological history. One of the Christian remains had been buried in a shroud showing a distorted image of the dead person's face, similar to the image on Shroud of Turin. A detailed analysis of the Shroud's image led experts to conclude that it had in fact been made by a chemical process involving spices. This enabled academics to view the Turin Shroud in a completely different way, and because of this and other similar burial cloths that have been unearthed, some experts have categorically stated that the Shroud of Turin is most definitely genuine and could not have been faked.

The Seamless Robe

The seamless robe was the garment that Jesus was wearing when he was taken to be crucified. It was so-called because it was woven in one piece, without a seam. Because of the unusual way the robe was woven, the Roman soldiers watching over Jesus on the cross cast lots for it. It has been suggested that Helena, the mother of Constantine the Great, discovered the robe in the Holy Land in the year 327 along with several other artifacts belonging to Jesus, including the actual cross he was crucified on. One version of this story is that she bequeathed it to the city of Trier where her son had lived for some years before becoming Emperor. The robe was allegedly kept folded in a reliquary and could not be viewed by anyone. In 1512, Archbishop Richard von Greiffenklau exhibited the relic in the presence of Emperor Maximilian 1, as a result of which pilgrimages took place to see the garment right up until 1996, and in that year over one million pilgrims allegedly viewed the seamless robe of Jesus.

As with all religious relics, confusion arises with yet another seamless robe that is preserved in a crypt in the Patriarchal Svetitskhoveli Cathedral, Misketa, Georgia, and which is claimed is a garment that was worn by Jesus when he was crucified. The authenticity of the robe was purported to have been attested by Nectarius, Archbishop of Vologda, by Patriarch Theophanes of Jerusalem, and also by Joannicius the Greek. It was claimed that miraculous signs worked through the robe.

Garment of Young Jesus

Yet another garment belonging to Jesus was moved to the church of Argenteuil in 1895. Although this garment was originally thought to be the robe worn by Jesus when he was crucified, it was later believed to be the garment that was woven by his mother Mary, when he was a child and which was worn by him for most of his young life. According to some sources, the Empress Irene made a gift of the seamless robe to Charlemagne in about the year 800. He gave it to his daughter Theocrate, Abbess of Argenteuil, where it was believed to have been preserved in the church of the Benedictines. Unfortunately, in 1793, the parish priest, afraid that the robe would be destroyed in the French Revolution, cut it into pieces and secreted them away in different places. Only four pieces of the garment are believed to have survived.

The authenticity of many relics purporting to have belonged to Jesus have been proved to be modern forgeries, a viable business in Eastern countries. Nonetheless, even experts sometimes have great difficulty in ascertaining whether or not some artifacts are genuine.

Chapter Six

Jesus and Mary Magdalene

Where exactly the suggestion actually originated that Mary Magdalene was a prostitute is not quite clear, as it is also believed that she was born of royal heritage in the Palace of Magdala, literally meaning the 'high tower'. Magdala was actually two miles north of the city of Tiberius, along the lakeshore on the Sea of Galilee. This was an extremely thriving agricultural, fishing and general trade location, visited by commercial travelers from all over, and was the home of many wealthy traders. Mary Magdalene's father was named Cyrus, King of the Benjamite tribe. In fact, each of the twelve tribes of Israel had a king, and Cyrus was an extremely wise and well-loved ruler, respected by all who knew him. Mary Magdalene's mother was called Eucharis, and her brother was Lazarus, the man whom Jesus raised from the dead, as mentioned in the New Testament. Her sister, Martha, also mentioned in the New Testament, was very close to Mary, and as children they were inseparable. It was clear to Mary Magdalene's family from the very beginning that she was quite special and had been 'chosen' to take a particular pathway in life. She was highly intelligent and well educated in the scriptures, a prerequisite for someone who would share Jesus' life and work alongside him.

There is now much evidence to support the suggestions that Mary Magdalene became one of the disciples of Jesus, and was in fact very close to him. Like Jesus, it is said that she was extremely charismatic and gifted with metaphysical abilities. Whilst Jesus was known to be an extremely affectionate and tactile man, some reports have stated that he was frequently seen kissing Mary Magdalene on the lips, and that this made some of his disciples very jealous. This obvious show of affection also caused a great deal of unrest amongst his followers, who were frequently heard saying that this was not the behavior of a Messiah. One theory that has even been accepted as a little more than a possibility, is that while Jesus was staying in Yusu Margh on route to Kashmir on the suggestion of the king there, he allegedly married Mary Magdalene. Although Jesus and Mary Magdalene obviously had a deep love for each other, it was suggested that their marriage would perpetuate the royal bloodline of Jesus.

Although there are various writings that suggest that Mary Magdalene and Jesus had several children, they most definitely had at the very least four, two boys and two girls. If, as many scholars have suggested, Jesus and Mary only had one child — a daughter, then the bloodline of Jesus would have been distorted and not fully perpetuated. The eldest child was a girl called Sarah, a very beautiful child who was intellectually advanced for her years. Like the young Jesus, their daughter was believed to be special and extremely gifted spiritually. In some parts of Southern France she is known as Saint Sarah, particularly to the gypsies. However, although she is their patron saint, they do deny that she was the daughter of Jesus, even though there seems to be enough evidence to support this theory. In the same parts of France, there are stories of Mary Magdalene arriving on their shores accompanied by a young girl, her sister, Martha, and her brothers. Although many of these stories contradict each other, they all seem to agree that Mary Magdalene arrived on the shores of France with other refugees from Palestine. Of course, a lot of confusion regarding Mary Magdalene has arisen from Dan Brown's bestselling book, *The Da Vinci Code*, and the *Holy Blood and the Holy Grail* by the authors, Michael Baigent, Richard Leigh and Henry Lincoln. Nonetheless, although the authors of the above mentioned books have been accused of creating a chiefly fictitious account of the whole story of Jesus and Mary Magdalene, such literary works have sufficed to catch the imagination of the Christian world, thus bringing attention to the greatest conspiracy of all time. Although the authors' hypothesis that Mary Magdalene travelled with her daughter to what is now known as Southern France, was intended as a work of fiction, they have unknowingly stumbled upon something that has been well documented in ancient writings for 2000 years.

There are in fact numerous accounts suggesting that once Jesus had fully recovered from his extremely traumatic ordeal of the crucifixion, he appeared to his disciples as they were having a meal (Mark 16:9, 14). They were apparently all amazed to see that he was still alive, but Thomas doubted that it was he, thinking that standing before them was the spirit body of Jesus. In the biblical narration of the event, Jesus showed his disciples the wounds on his hands and feet and invited them to touch them. As mentioned in an earlier chapter, he even ate a piece of broiled fish and honeycomb in order to prove that it was really him and not a spirit, as they thought (Luke, 24:39–43). Jesus said, 'A spirit hath not bones and flesh as ye see me have'.

It had become quite apparent that because of a dream Pilate's wife had had about Jesus, he wanted to save him. This was probably the reason he released his body for safekeeping into the hands of Joseph of Arimathea, believed to be the uncle of Jesus. Word was spreading that Jesus had not died and before leaving his disciples, he instructed them to carry on his good work, thereby perpetuating the sacred cause.

Although Jesus travelled incognito under the name of Yuz Asaph, in each country he travelled through he was known by different names. Accompanied by a small group of devotees, it is thought that Jesus revisited the countries he had been taken to by the Magi as a young boy, and stayed for a short while at the various monasteries and lodges. This time though he and his followers were made welcome, and it is said that the priests and leading monastic teachers were enthralled by his teachings, which obviously made him stand apart from other religious teachers. A detailed study of the way Jesus taught led experts to conclude that his teaching were not those usually propagated through Judaic tradition, but seemed to follow more a Buddhist line of thought. As Buddhism was five hundred years older than Christianity, there was in fact one suggestion that Jesus was a Buddhist Master, and that the Three Wise Men may in fact have sought him out to take his place as the great Lama, in accordance with Buddhist tradition. Comparisons have also been made between Jesus, Buddha and Lord Krishna, whose lives all ran a similar vein. It has also been suggested that Jesus was a practitioner of yoga, which is why he was able to perform such magnificent feats as walking on water, turning water into wine and even healing, all of which are known in the yogic tradition as *Siddhis* (perfect abilities). These psychic or supernatural skills are achieved by the most highly developed and disciplined yogic masters.

As we have already earlier established it was Jesus' mission to gather the lost tribes of Israel, and to bring his people back to the spirit of truth. Although the lost tribes of Israel were believed to have been scattered far and wide, Jesus eventually located a good part of these in the valley of Srinagar in Kashmir. It was here that he eventually settled, and for a time lived on a mountaintop overlooking the valley.

Due to the fact that after the crucifixion Jesus was known by various names, confusion appears to have cast a huge shadow over the story of his life in Kashmir. This confusion has perhaps come about as a result of the innumerable interpretations made by religious scholars and other writers over the years about the life of Jesus beyond the crucifixion. As well as the name Yuz Asaph, he appears also to have been known as Isa-Masihas, meaning *'Jesus the Messiah'*. Even the actual meaning of the name Yuz Asaph seems to vary from writing to writing. Some writers on the subject translate the name Yuz Asaph as literally meaning 'Jesus the Gatherer', whilst others say that it means 'Jesus the

Prophet of Israel'. The word Yuz is another form of Yuyu, meaning Jesus in the Old Persian language, or Yasu, Jesus in Persian as well as in the Arabic translated from the Greek. Therefore, the word Yuz means Jesus and Asaph is the biblical name meaning *collector* or *gatherer*, or one who was to gather the lost tribes of Israel. In the Holy Quran, Jesus is referred to as *Isa*, the shortened form of the Hebrew word *Ishu*. Whatever name Jesus was known by, there is little doubt now that he did survive the crucifixion and lived on to a great age.

Jesus was also known locally as 'Issa the White Saint' and as soon as the word spread about his miraculous powers the sick and lame came from far and wide to receive healing from Him. He spoke in parables, and referred to his preaching as *Bushra* (Gospel), and was frequently heard comparing his disciples to birds. When a comparison is made between the biblical teachings of Jesus, and those expounded by Yuz Asaph in Srinagar, the similarities are unquestionable.

Mary Magdalene Leaves

Mary Magdalene was considerably younger than Jesus and was fully aware from the very beginning of the part she was to play in the Messianic mission alongside her husband. Although there has been an exhaustive study of the life of Mary Magdalene, most of what has been written about her has been speculation and the writer's attempt at filling in the missing pieces of this fascinating mystery. Even though I am well aware that my attempt at presenting yet another theory might well be regarded as the same as all the others, the version I am offering is the results of many years of studying the subject.

Once Jesus was fully established in Srinagar, he decided that his wife, Mary, should continue her work as his number one disciple, even though this would involve her leaving him. By this time, the four children of Mary Magdalene and Jesus were fully aware of exactly how important their father was. Although Jesus had seen to it that his children had all been well educated in the various esoteric traditions, it was in fact Sarah, the eldest who excelled and showed an exceptional talent for mastering both the text and the spoken word. At this time, Sarah was 12 years old, extremely advanced for her years and very gifted just as her father had been when he was that age. Although Jesus had seen to it that all his children had been brought up according to Judaic tradition, each one showed an aptitude for the teachings of Buddha, and the oldest boy exhibited an exceptional talent for the disciplines of yoga. However, it was Sarah who excelled and somehow mastered all she had been taught with great ease. She appeared quite 'special' in comparison to her siblings and possessed that certain 'fire' and determination to carry on her father's work alongside her mother. It is believed that even at the age of eight she was capable of holding long discussions with the elders of the temple in Srinagar, again like her father had done when he was young, and even astounded them by quoting their own religious texts verbatim. Therefore, it was clear to Mary Magdalene that Sarah must accompany her on her travels towards Southern France.

Although as I have already stated the story of Mary Magdalene landing in France with a very young daughter was brought to the attention of the world in the bestselling books of some modern-day writers, it is known that by the time their small ship had reached the shores of France, Sarah was in fact thirteen and a half years old. The reason for the trip was primarily to transport certain artifacts of great Messianic significance to ensure their safekeeping, and to convey the sacred word of Jesus to other lands, thereby perpetuating the Christian message. It had been arranged for the mother and daughter to stay in a monastery in Narbonne where they rested after their long journey. The monastic brothers here were overwhelmed with the excitement of having such important visitors, especially with the artifacts they had brought with them. There have been suggestions that Mary Magdalene also carried with her the Sacred Chalice used at the Last Supper, and which has now become known as the *Holy Grail*. Although there is quite a lot of controversy about whether or not the Holy Grail even existed, the majority of academics seem to agree that it did but that it was not a cup but a core of sacred teachings, the key to which was in fact Mary Magdalene and her daughter, Sarah. A great deal of evidence has also surfaced to suggest that the real Holy Grail was in fact an extremely unusual iridescent stone, the substance of which was allegedly from a planet far removed from this world. The stone, referred to as Mary Magdalene's *Shining Stone of the Soul* is believed to be priceless and lies somewhere in Southern France. This stone gave rise to yet another bizarre theory that Jesus and Mary Magdalene may have even been extraterrestrial in origin, which some believed would account for their miraculous powers. Even with all this conflicting evidence, over the years other pieces of evidence have come to light about the Sacred Chalice completely contradicting this narrative and adding even more confusion to the whole story of the Holy Grail. Some religious scholars have even suggested that Mary Magdalene herself may have been the Holy Grail, and that she most probably played a much bigger part in the story of Christianity, than previously suggested in the biblical narrative.

As we now know, there are many legends about the Sacred Chalice. One particular account is quite interesting, and suggests that Joseph of Arimathea caught some of Jesus' blood in it as he was being taken down from the cross. This is supposed to have given the chalice many mystical properties that would be passed on to anyone fortunate to possess it. Joseph allegedly took the chalice to Britain where it is suggested he spent the rest of his life. The cup furnished Joseph with food, drink and spiritual support. The Sacred Chalice allegedly then passed from Joseph to his descendants who had settled in Glastonbury and parts of Cornwall. Because of the sinfulness of its keepers, it is believed to have disappeared completely from view.

The story of the Holy Grail is interwoven with those of King Arthur and the Knights of the Round Table. The search for the Sacred Chalice was the object of many knightly adventures. It is believed that only the pure in heart might ever find it, but it is said that three of Arthur's knights actually saw it and were able to hold it. These were Galahad, Perceval and Bors.

The Great Chalice of Antioch

In 1910, some Arab workmen were excavating the ruins of the Cathedral of Antioch (built by Constantine the Great,) when they discovered a precious goblet. It was of carved silver covered with gold leaf, and had an inner cup of plain metal. The goblet is called the Great Chalice of Antioch and is thought to be the cup from which Jesus drank at the Last Supper. The workmen sold the goblet to the Kouchakjii family, Syrian art dealers of Paris for an undisclosed sum of money. Many experts were unsure of the origins of the religious artifact and were therefore understandably reluctant to confirm that it was genuine. However, there were some arguments based primarily on its peculiar physical condition, which did appeal to most of the archaeologists who had seen it. These included Dr Edward Robinson of the Metropolitan Museum of Art, and authority on Christian monuments, Josef Strzygowski, who were suspicious of religious artifacts that come out of anonymous holes in the ground. They went on to say that 'few objects that have come to light in recent times offer so many questions for dispute and decision as the Great Chalice of Antioch, which those who have the will to believe will even identify as the Holy Grail'.

In 1936, the Sacred Chalice was in the hands of Mr Fahim Kouchakjii and was kept in the vaults at his home.

The goblet can be seen today in the Metropolitan Museum in New York City.

Chapter Seven

Jesus and the Mystery Teachings

Although some religious scholars totally dismiss the suggestion that there is a secret or hidden side of Christianity, the truth is that religion as we know it today is made up of the remnants of a core of teachings that were once known as the *'Mysteries'* and which could only be given by teacher to pupil, mouth to ear. In fact, this recondite knowledge — the Mystery Teachings, are to some degree the very foundation upon which religion as we know it today is based, and the early Christian Fathers were desperate to conceal the truth, for fear that this would give the ordinary people far too much spiritual and intellectual power, and in so doing take away the power that they themselves possessed.

For 2000 years, Christians have been misled about the life and death of Jesus, and today theologians have built up such a powerful screen of dogmatic theory around the Christian doctrine, that only when we dig deep enough can we hope to discover the *truth* about God, Life and the Universe. Because these teachings have for thousands of years lain beneath the incredible mound of falsehood created by the church and the early Christians, the onus is now on the shoulders of those who seek the truth to distinguish what is genuine from what is not. For many this is a difficult task and relies solely upon the inherent knowledge that arises from the very depths of the seeker's soul. The knowledge that has somehow filtered through over the last 2000 years is labeled the 'Lesser Mysteries' or the exoteric teachings for the masses, and although the 'Greater Mysteries', the esoteric teachings containing the *truth* cannot be written down, the 'Lesser Mysteries' can and may easily be discovered today in books and other writings in all religious cultures.

As we have previously discussed, Jesus received most of his education from the Essenes who took it upon themselves to carefully cultivate the mind of the one they believed would carry the occult flame and bring the orthodox Jews back to the spirit of truth. The Essenes had three orders in the communities: the Neophytes, the Brethren and the Perfect. The Perfect were the initiates, and the Essenes referred to the candidate who had just been initiated as 'The Little Child' or as they would say, the one who had just taken his second birth. The 'second birth' is a well recognized term for initiation in esoteric circles, and even in India today the higher castes are sometimes referred to as 'twice-born', whereby they are subjected to a ceremony of initiation. The biblical narration of Jesus' conversation with Nicodemus illustrates this 'second-birth' of initiation perfectly, when Jesus said, 'Except a man be born again, he cannot see the kingdom of God' (John 3:3). The first Initiation referred to as 'Water and the Spirit' appears in the Gospel according to John(3:5) and is symbolic of the birth and welcomes the 'Little Child' into the Kingdom. A later initiation is the 'Holy Ghost and Fire' (Matt. 3:11) and symbolizes the actual baptism of the initiate into manhood. In the biblical account of the conversation Jesus had with Nicodemus, Jesus was surprised that the priest did not understand his mystical use of words, 'Art thou a master of Israel, and knowest not these things?' (John 3:10).

Jesus also confused his disciples with another reference to one of the final degrees of initiation, 'Be ye therefore perfect, even as your Father which is in heaven is perfect' (Matt. 5:48). Jesus was obviously surprised that his disciples had not understood the esoteric meaning of initiation but had taking his words literally, knowing that what Jesus was asking of them was impossible. Jesus was referring to 'perfect' in the final degree of initiation and did not intend them to take his words literally.

Once we are familiar with the Essenic terms of initiation we can then comprehend more fully the biblical passages which bear a direct reference to the process of initiation, such as, 'Then said one unto Him: Lord, are there few that be saved? And he said unto them: Strive to enter in at the strait gate; for many, I say unto you, will seek to enter in and shall not be able' (Luke 13:23–24). The biblical intimation is no doubt extremely misleading, and refers to someone avoiding hell but finding it difficult to enter heaven. Looked at from the esoteric perspective it is clear that the narrow gate in the passage is a direct reference to the Gate of Initiation. The passage goes on to say, 'Enter ye in at the strait gate; for wide is the gate and broad is the way that leadeth to destruction, and many there be which go in there at; because strait is the gate and narrow is the way which leadeth unto life; and few there be that find it' (Matt. 7:13). There were in fact several terms used to described the way to initiation, one of which was 'The Strait Gate', another that is mentioned in the passage above is 'The Narrow Path', both of these were direct references to initiation. The *Ancient Narrow Way* is known to all students of esoteric traditions; the path to knowledge and enlightenment being extremely difficult to tread and is rocky and uneven, or perhaps sharp like the edge of a knife. 'The Strait Gate' is obviously the Gateway of Initiation and through this, the candidate entered the 'Kingdom' — a reference perhaps to the secret knowledge itself. The early Christian Fathers viewed the following passage as a reference to the secret teachings, which in fact it was, but perhaps not in exactly the way they thought: 'Give not that which is holy to the dogs, neither cast ye your pearls before swine' (Matt. 7:6). This precept most probably refers to imparting the secret knowledge or the Mysteries to those who were not spiritually equipped to understand it, or to those who perhaps understood it but would only misuse it for their own ends.

There is very little doubt that Jesus could only pass on the

Mystery Teachings to those of his disciples who he knew were ready to be initiated, and this is made clear in the passage: 'I have yet many things to say to you, but ye cannot bear them now' (John 16:12), he also said to his disciples, 'Unto you it is given to know the Mystery of the Kingdom of God, but unto them that are without, all these things are done in parables'(Luke 8:10). This passage clearly indicates that Jesus conveyed the Lesser Mysteries or exoteric teachings in parables to those who were not ready, and the literal meaning of the Greater Mysteries or esoteric teachings to those he knew would understand them.

Jesus the Mystic

The existence of a recondite knowledge or secret doctrine has been known from as far back in antiquity as we can go. This doctrine was carefully guarded by the Masters of Wisdom whose job it was to instruct those who were suitable candidates for initiation into 'The Mysteries', as I have already explained above, the term used to describe the deepest and most profound aspects of religion, philosophy and science. In fact, the Mysteries were a core of teachings that formed the very basis of all that there was to be known about the deepest facts of man's origin, his true nature and connection with supersensual worlds and beings, as well as of course with the natural laws of the physical world. Every great teacher from time immemorial has passed through The Mysteries and been subjected to the tests and trials of initiation, thereby proving their worthiness of such an exalted position. Needless to say, few there were who were spiritually and morally equipped sufficiently to see initiation through to the very end. Many fell by the wayside and were cast out in shame. The very greatest of those who possessed what was required became the Hierophants of the Mysteries, and were considered highly evolved spiritually with the arduous task of ensuring that the sacred teachings did not fall into the hands of the wrong people. They had to keep the occult flame burning and, in so doing, protected the Mystery Teachings as though they were gold. A minority of those who were successfully initiated prostituted their abilities to suit their own ends, and to gain recognition as teachers in their own right. These were branded 'Teachers of the Black Arts' and driven underground where they established their own secret groups, many of which are still in existence today.

Jesus was undoubtedly a very highly evolved soul and someone who knew from a very early age the importance of the life that lay ahead of him. As I explained above Jesus had been educated in his early years by members of the elite monastic sect, the Essenes, themselves in full possession of what had become known as the *'Gnostic teachings'*. The Essenes had prior knowledge of Jesus' birth and had been appointed to take care of his training and even though these monastic guardians of Jesus were said to be hard taskmasters, they found it very difficult to control him. Jesus was extremely headstrong and possessed his own fixed ideas as to what religion was all about and what exactly should be done to bring the Judaic peoples back to the spirit of truth. In this regard, Jesus had no intention of being anything other than a spiritual teacher within the confines of Judaism, and had never at any time set his sights on being a Messiah to the masses. However, it was clear that the Essenes had other ideas for him, and it was these ideas against which Jesus protested very strongly.

It is easy to understand then how someone with so much charismatic power and spiritual knowledge attracted such a large following. He was without a doubt an extremely excellent orator and was able to infuse his words with immense mystical power thus captivating those who listened to him preaching. Jesus had been educated in numerous esoteric traditions and had also taken pains to cultivate and refine those mystical powers about which the Bible speaks, albeit very briefly. There is in fact a great deal of evidence to suggest that not only was Jesus well versed in the traditions of Buddhism, but he was also a yogic master of the highest kind, and was frequently seen demonstrating his mystical powers (Siddhis) to his many followers. As a result of the innumerable people who came to see him from miles around, he is thought to have established an ashram on the mountain top where he lived in Srinagar. In fact, the news that Jesus had settled in Srinagar quickly spread. He was not only visited by his passionate devotees, but a ransom that had been placed on his head also attracted those who sought only to make a name for themselves by capturing or even assassinating him. However, it is believed that once the enemies of Jesus where actually in his presence, they too were so overwhelmed by his mystical and charismatic powers, that they also became loyal followers, remaining on the ashram to learn from the wisdom of his teachings.

As previously stated, the tradition of a recondite knowledge has been recorded throughout all ages in antiquity. The esoteric side of this knowledge was especially for the *few*, whilst the masses could only be given the exoteric version of the teachings, which they were capable of understanding. Once one was ready to receive the esoteric or secret doctrine, they would have to then be subjected to the appropriate tests and trials thereby proving their worthiness. Although as I have already stated that this knowledge was very generally known under the term of 'the Mysteries', the label used to describe the secret teachings is as meaningful today as it was when it was very first created. As no other term could suitably be used the 'Mysteries' is still the most effective way of describing those ancient teachings that Jesus expounded to the 'chosen' few 2000 years ago and which today still silently underlies modern day Christianity. The Mystery Teachings were primarily concerned with the deepest facts of man's origins, his spiritual nature, and connection with super-sensual worlds and beings, as well as that is with the natural laws of the physical world.

Jesus had long since proved that he was a master of the highest kind and had been initiated long before he had begun his ministry. It is said that whilst living in Srinagar he was also known as the *White Saint* who lived on the mountaintop overlooking the valley. He was a man of peace and righteousness and devoted most of his time to prayer and meditation and to educating his people in the traditions of Buddha.

Jesus had resigned himself to the fact that he would never see his wife Mary Magdalene again. In accordance with Messianic tradition, Mary's path had taken her in a completely different direction. In fact, Mary too had been anointed as one who had to walk the path of the Messiah, and to ensure that the word of her husband would be perpetuated in foreign lands. Even with all this information, one other theory posed by religious scholars is that Mary Magdalene did not leave her husband, but that she sent her daughter, Sarah with her closest friend, Miriam, a Kashmiri woman, to the South of France. This is where confusion arises as to the life of Mary Magdalene. The truth is we are left to draw our own conclusions from the information available to us. Nonetheless, it is my opinion that Mary Magdalene did leave for the South of France with her daughter, and that she was most probably accompanied by her close friend, Miriam. We must also remember that Mary was of royal blood, and although she was of a different faith to Jesus, she did uphold the Mosaic Law, in accordance with Judaic tradition. Jesus was the last prophet in Israel, a firm believer in Moses and all the prophets of Israel who followed after him. Jesus was himself bound by the Mosaic Law and abided by it. He was the heir to the throne of David and was to reign over the house of Jacob (Luke 1: 32-33). And although he intended his ministry as a prophet to be confined to the children of Israel, his many followers obviously had other plans for him.

One thing has to be made clear and this is that the secret doctrine of Christianity did not originate with Jesus, for he himself was an initiate of the Mysteries, which had been taught hundreds of years before he was born. St Augustine said, 'That which is called the Christian Religion existed among the ancients and never did not exist, from the beginning of the human race until Christ came in the flesh, at which time the true religion which already existed began to be called Christianity'.

It is now clear to the majority of religious scholars that Christianity has long since forgotten much of its original teachings, and today only puts forth a very small part of what it knew in the very beginning. Although today the scriptures appear intrinsically the same, they indicate that there is more to know! However, that *more*, whatever it was has been lost completely to the church and its priests. St Paul used a well-known technical term for men at a certain stage of initiation when he said, 'We speak wisdom among them which are perfect'. It has also been said of this wisdom and those who are ready to receive it, 'When the student is ready the teacher will appear'. It's an extremely bizarre fact that it is only Christianity that is blind to the truth about the life and death of Jesus. All Eastern traditions are in full possession of the facts, and these are that Jesus was a supreme master and the possessor of incredible supernatural abilities. These facts along with the knowledge that Jesus did not die on the cross but travelled incognito to many countries, eventually to settle in Srinagar and live on to a ripe old age, are known to all non-Christian countries. Little wonder then why Christianity has not evolved at all but in fact has taken a backward step. The majority of Christians are appalled at the very suggestion that Jesus did not die on the cross to save the world, and that he married Mary Magdalene and had children, thereby perpetuating the royal bloodline of Jesus. This now seems to be far more than speculation and it is a very controversial topic that has been the subject of innumerable bestselling books.

Chapter Eight

The Tomb of Jesus

It is easy to understand exactly why Jesus chose Srinagar as the place to live out the rest of his life. It is the floating capital of Kashmir and also referred to in Deuteronomy 11:11 as 'Paradise on Earth'. It is set in a backdrop of hills and valleys that 'drinketh the rain of heaven'. Thomas had been a constant companion of Jesus and it has always been suggested that he was the twin brother of Jesus. Since Mary Magdalene had left for France, Jesus came to rely more and more on his brother, and together they continued to preach not only in Srinagar, but also in neighboring towns. Of the remaining three children of Jesus, only the girl remained with him. Her two brothers had married, and she and her husband had remained in the ashram with Jesus along with the few remaining devotees. Jesus was now reaching the end of his life and preparations had to be made for his burial. He instructed Thomas as to where exactly he was to be buried, and said to him, 'My time for departing this world has come. Carry on your duties properly and turn not back from truth, and say your prayers regularly'. And then surrounded by his children and a handful of his devotees, Jesus lay down with his head turned towards the north and his face to the east, and then he died.

As Jesus had instructed Thomas erected a simple tomb exactly where his body lay. The tomb is to be found today situated in Anzimar, Khanyar, Srinagar, the summer capital of Kashmir. Although the city is divided into two parts, the tomb is situated in the old city. The people of Kashmir call the tomb of Jesus the Rozabal, meaning 'the site of the honored tomb', and proclaim the sepulchre as the tomb of Yuz Asaph, who came to live in Kashmir approximately 2000 years ago. The popular local tradition has always been that the tomb is that of Jesus Christ, 'the Prophet of the People of the Book'. The Rozabal contains two graves; one of the prophet, Yuz Asaph, and the other a descendant of the prophet of Islam, Nazir-ud-Din. Sahibzada Basharat Saleem, a writer and respected healer living in Srinagar, is a direct descendant of Jesus. According to tradition, his family have always been charged with the maintenance of the Rozabal, the sepulchre of Jesus. It is recorded that Basharat Saleem's own father was also a respected healer in Srinagar and was known to have brought more than one person back from the point of death with his healing. Although Sahibzada Basharat Saleem has been interviewed by many writers over the years, it is said of him that he does not seek publicity or fame, and lives a quiet life writing poetry.

The Tomb of Moses

The alleged tomb of Moses is located on Mount Niltopp, approximately 38 miles north-west of Srinagar. A small Jewish community can be found near the tomb of Moses, and it is they who have taken it upon themselves to look after the burial place of their ancestral leader. In a place named Aishmuqam, on a route into Kashmir can be found an extremely significant religious artifact, and that is the Staff of Moses — also known as the Staff of Jesus. Locals believe that the staff once belonged to Jesus and that it was handed down to him in accordance with Messianic tradition. The staff made of dark brown olive wood, measures eight feet three inches long, and from one and a quarter to one and three quarter inches in diameter. The staff is also known as Balagir, meaning 'the preventer of calamities', and is carefully preserved and kept under lock and key in a sanctuary in Aishmuqam. The locals also believe that the staff possesses mystical powers and that it has caused it to rain when there has been drought, and protected them from other natural disasters such as earthquakes, and even the plague.

Many ancient legends and traditions about Moses can be found throughout Kashmir, one of which is about the Stone of Moses(Sang-i-Musa), which is located in Bijibhara, close to a fast-flowing river where Moses allegedly bathed. The stone is known locally as Ka Ka Pal. It weighs approximately 108 pounds, and it is believed that if eleven people each place one finger on the lower part of the stone, and then chant simultaneously 'Ka Ka Ka Ka Ka Ka', the stone will lose its weight and may then be lifted with ease. This incredible feat can only be achieved when the correct number of people is involved in the lifting process.

It is quite clear that the whole area of Kashmir lies beneath an incredible mantel of spiritual mystery, and that not only did Jesus seek the lost tribes there, but he was also aware that Moses was buried there. This in itself had some mystical significance.

Although the Virgin Birth was not a part of the original teachings, and is only mentioned very briefly in Mathew and Luke, there are remarkable similarities between the birth of Jesus and the birth of Buddha. Just like Mary, the mother of Jesus, Buddha's mother is also believed to have been a virgin when she gave birth to him. There is a consensus of opinion that Jesus was greatly influenced by Buddhism, and reflected this in his teachings. However, some schools of religious thought now firmly believe that Buddhism was in actual fact influenced by the teachings of Jesus. Gautama Buddha had apparently said that his successor would be fair-skinned, and Jesus fitted perfectly into that prediction. There are indeed innumerable similarities between the life of Buddha and the life of Jesus. For example, Buddha travelled to Benares, where he performed miracles and gave a sermon on the mount, just like the biblical narrative of Jesus. There are also similarities between Jesus and Buddha in the way to which they are referred. Buddha, which means 'The Enlightened One' is more or less the same as the way in which Jesus refers to himself as 'The Light of the World', (John 8:12). Whilst Buddha was called 'Sasta' by his disciples, Jesus was called 'Master', which means the same thing. Jesus and Buddha were referred to as both 'Prince' and 'King', and Jesus was called 'the refuge of the weary' and Buddha 'the refuge of those who have no shelter'. The similarities are too many to recount here, but there is very little doubt that there is a connection between the two great teachers. It has been suggested that when Jesus arrived in India for the second time (the first being when he was a young boy) that the Buddhists there were already familiar with the teachings he had left on his first visit and so believed that he was the long awaited Messiah. It has also been suggested that the literary details of Buddha's life only began to be recorded during the lifetime of Jesus, and so the Buddhist priests really had a free hand and could have ascribed to Buddha anything they wanted. In fact, this may have been where all the confusion arose and where the connection between the two exalted teachers was made. Nonetheless, there is a common thread running through the teachings of Buddha and Jesus who both expounded philosophies of virtue and righteousness.

Primarily because of the similarities between the life of Jesus and Buddha, some religious scholars believed that Jesus' tomb, the Rozabal, actually contained the body of Buddha. Buddha died at Kusinagara in Oude at the age of 80, in 543 BC, and his remains were deposited in a number of monumental tombs to preserve them. Had the entombed person been Gautama Buddha or any other Hindu raja, saint or prince, the sepulchre would have been owned and visited by Buddhists and Hindus. Yuz Asaph is a Hebrew name and it could not in any way be taken for another form of Budistava. Although many religious scholars have questioned the identity of the person entombed in the Rozabal, it has now been positively established that it contains the remains of Yuz Asaph of Kashmir, known to many as *Jesus the Prophet of the People of the Book*.

Saint Thomas in India

After the death of Jesus at the ripe old age of 120 years old, there appears to be some discrepancies in the life of Thomas from then on. It is thought that Thomas remained with Jesus until his death, after which time he left Srinagar as Jesus had instructed, and went to Malabar to preach to the lost tribes there. If this is so then Thomas himself must have been a reasonable age, and most probably far too old to travel. Regardless of whether or not he remained with Jesus until his death, one thing is clear, and that is that Thomas continued to preach the Gospel to the people in Southern India where it is alleged he established seven churches. Remember, Thomas was the doubter and did not believe that Jesus was still alive. It was only when Jesus showed him the wounds in his side and those inflicted by the nails that Thomas was convinced that he was still alive. Whatever happened, we know for certain that Thomas eventually suffered martyrdom at Mylapore in Madras where his tomb can be found today.

Thomas was known as the evangelist of 'Parthia' it has been suggested probably because Edessa where some of his bones were preserved is sometimes called 'Edessa of Parthia'. It is believed that Thomas's bones were brought to Edessa from India, and a work known as the *Acts of Thomas* highlights his work as a missionary and eventual martyrdom in India. In fact, the *Acts of Thomas* is a detailed example of earliest Christianity in the countries east of the Euphrates. It is interesting to note that that this work refers to the apostle as Judah Thomas and clearly states that he was the twin of Jesus Christ. The Acts is clearly a historical account of Thomas's work in southern India and explains that the ancient Christian churches found there are referred to as 'Christians of St Thomas'. Thomas founded the Christian churches in Malabar, the south-west coast, and then travelled into Malabar, today a suburb of Madras, where in 1547 the Portuguese rebuilt the shrine of Thomas's martyrdom, and which is still there to this very day.

The oldest Christian site in the world is the Syro-Malankaran, whose followers claim that the first residents there were baptized by St Thomas himself when he arrived on their coast in approximately AD 59. It is further alleged that he bestowed upon them the name Nazarenes, long before the term had ever been used in this way. There has always been a little doubt as to whether Thomas visited India at all, but researchers studying the life of Thomas have concluded that the legend is based on too much historical fact for it to be dismissed. He was eventually martyred by the Brahmins, and his relics are kept in the Cathedral at Mylapore near Madras, and which is dedicated to his name.

There is very little doubt that Thomas fulfilled the duties given to him by Jesus who said, 'Go rather to the Lost Sheep of the House of Israel'.

As I have previously said, although Jesus' ministry in Palestine lasted only a few years there are over 800 million Christians in the world today. However, even though Jesus is said to have spent approximately 80 years of his life in the north-western part of India, he left no trace of his teachings there.

Chapter Nine

Miscellaneous — Buddha and Jesus

Although the life of Jesus after the crucifixion is enshrouded in mystery, at least where the Western Christian world is concerned, to all Eastern religious cultures his physical survival has been common knowledge since the actual event, and is even today an integral part of their traditions. The fact that Jesus was still alive had to be a closely guarded secret, as there were fears that he would be caught and crucified a second time. Some documents indicate that after the crucifixion Jesus departed from Judea and travelled north and visited Damascus. There was a large Jewish community in and around Damascus, which was most probably the primary reason he wanted to remain there for a while. While Jesus was there, he converted many of his persecutors into disciples. One of these was Saul, who intended to capture Jesus to be crucified a second time. Jesus confronted him and Saul was said to be overwhelmed by his powerful charisma, causing his conversion into a disciple. Word was quickly spreading that Jesus was still alive and a reward was offered for his capture. It was clearly not safe for him to remain in Damascus so he then headed towards Babylon towards the east and stayed for a while at Nasibain, a short distance from Mosul. There are clear indications that Jesus entered Iran en-route to Afghanistan. He also stayed for a short while in Herat, a town near the border of Afghanistan. As I have said in a previous chapter, there is a plateau in Iran with an inscription marking the place where Jesus taught. From Afghanistan, Jesus made his way to India where he also taught for a while, before making his way to Kashmir, the place in which he always intended to settle.

Scattered around the western parts of Afghanistan can be

found the followers of Isa — Jesus the son of Mary — many of whom call themselves Moslems. It has been suggested by some scholars that they were in fact converted by European missionaries from Eastern Persia, or perhaps a relic of the time when Herat had been a flourishing bishopric of the Nestorian rite, before Persia was conquered by the Arabs in the seventh and eighth centuries. But according to the people themselves, their history originates further back. There are approximately a thousand or so of these Christians, the chief of which is the Abba Yahiyya (Father John) who is in full possession of the line of teachers going back nearly 60 generations to Isa — Jesus, the son of Mary. According to their traditions, Jesus escaped death on the cross, and was hidden by friends until he had fully recovered. Once his health was restored, he fled to India, and eventually settled in Kashmir.

The Afghans proclaim themselves to be the descendents of some of the lost tribes of Israel, and this tradition has been passed down through the ages. The names of several of the Afghan tribes strongly suggest that this is true. For example, Musa Khel, (the Tribe of Moses), Yusuf Zai, (the Tribe of Joseph), Daud Khel, (the Tribe of David), and Sulaiman Zai, (the Tribe of Solomon). In fact, a modern historical analysis of the Afghans has concluded that they are descended from the lost tribes of Israel, confirming suggestions that they settled in different parts of Afghanistan some time before the event of the crucifixion, and that Jesus did visit them and preached to them after his alleged death on the cross. This seems to be the general consensus of opinion amongst the various tribes of Afghanistan. The one-time Prime Minister of India, Pandit Jawaharlal Nehru, who was a Kashmiri Brahmin, is known to have said, 'All over Central Asia, in Kashmir, and Ladakh, and Tibet, and even further north, there is still a strong belief that Jesus, or Isa travelled about there ... There is nothing inherently improbable in his having done so' (from his book, *Glimpses of World History*).

It is common knowledge throughout the East that Jesus had converted to Buddhism and was a practitioner of its disciplines. An interesting fact highlighted by Sir Monier Williams in his book *Buddhism* is that the sixth disciple of the Buddha was a man named 'Yasa', a short version of 'Yasu', meaning Jesus. Although Jesus lived 500 years after the death of Buddha, he was frequently referred to as his sixth disciple. Whilst many religious scholars are agreed that Jesus was greatly influenced by the principles of Buddha, some argue that Buddhism may not have reached Palestine during the life of Jesus. Although it is clear from Buddhist texts that Yasu was the disciple of Buddha, it has also been suggested that this statement was most probably made by the priests of Buddhism to highlight the fact that a master who came much later was a disciple of the Buddha who came earlier. Although many investigators have tried to discover the historical evidence that the teachings of Buddhism did reach Palestine during the life of Jesus, the facts appear contradictory, even though there is very little doubt about Jesus' conversion to Buddhism after his crucifixion.

Dr Herman Oldenberg offered even more startling evidence in his book *Buddhism*. He maintains that various Buddhist texts taken from a book named *Mahawaga*, (page 54, section 1) also mention a man called 'Rahula' as being a disciple of Buddha as well as his son. One other writer believes that the 'Rahula' of Buddhist records is the corrupt form of 'Ruhullah', which is purported to be one of Jesus' titles. There are suggestions that Rahula is a reference to Jesus, whose other name is 'Ruhullah', which in Hebrew is similar to 'Rahula', the disciple of Buddha. And so, as the teachings of Jesus were in fact very similar to those of Buddha, even though he came 500 years after Buddha, Buddhist texts refer to him as a disciple of Buddha.

The lives of Jesus and Buddha bear uncanny mutual resemblances, even though these do not carry the respect and compassion we would expect from such exalted teachers. For example, it is mentioned in the Gospel that Jesus once showed no respect for his mother and that he did not care for her and even uttered insulting words to her. Buddha abandoned his son 'Rahula', when he was a baby and even walked out on his wife when she was asleep never to see her or his son ever again. These are not the actions of an enlightened being, but those of someone lacking compassion and human understanding and sensitivity for the feelings of others. This kind of behavior from such enlightened beings as Gautama Buddha and Jesus is most definitely offensive and contrary to their own teachings. Although these actions have been well documented they have obviously been recorded incorrectly and are most definitely wrong. In fact, there is such a striking resemblance between Buddha and Jesus that many Christian thinkers refer to Buddhism as the Christianity of the East, and Christianity the Buddhism of the West. Jesus is quoted as saying, 'I am the Light and the Way', and Buddha is also quoted as saying the same. The Gospels refer to Jesus as the Savior, and Buddha also calls himself the Savior. It is also mentioned in the Gospels that Jesus had no father, even though Joseph was his father. It is also stated in Buddhist texts that Buddha was born without a father, even though he did have a father. The biblical narration of the star appearing when Jesus was born is also a phenomenon that occurred when Buddha was born. The story of the two women who claimed to be the mother of a baby, and Solomon ordered the child to be cut in half and divided between them, is also found in Buddha's *Jataka*. This is yet another piece of evidence that Jesus travelled to India and Tibet and studied Buddhist literature, thus developing a relationship with Buddhism. It is also written that when Rahula was separated from his mother, a woman named Magdaliyana, a follower of Buddha acted as a messenger. The name Magdaliyana is a corrupt form of Magdalena, the name of Mary Magdalene who followed Jesus and eventually became his wife. There are far too many similarities between Jesus and Buddha to be coincidental; the facts speak for themselves. In fact, some ancient Tibetan texts assert that Jesus was actually born in India and that he studied Sanskrit Pali and read the Vedas and Buddhist Cannon. It further says that he then returned through Persia to Palestine to preach the Gospel. This was, of course, when he was a young man before the Crucifixion. However, there is quite a lot of evidence to support the suggestion that Jesus returned to Tibet after the crucifixion where he continued to study in the various esoteric lodges, en-route to Kashmir. As I have mentioned in an earlier chapter, Nicolas Notovitch, the writer and explorer, visited Tibet and was shown some ancient manuscripts in the Buddhist Monastery at Himis. The ancient text mentions at length Jesus' sojourn in Tibet. Nicolas Notovitch wrote about his experience in his book written in French, entitled *Vie inconnue de Jesus-Christ*, and published in 1894.

Notovitch was one of the first writers to point out the similarity between the teachings of Buddha and Jesus, and also to suggest that Jesus was greatly influenced by Buddhist doctrines, which in fact formed the basis of his own teachings. Nicolas Notovitch described the ancient documents as being written in Pali, the sacred language of Southern Buddhism, and that the information contained in the writings had most probably been dictated from the stories related by Jewish merchants who had travelled to India directly after the crucifixion. The ancient documents also contained parables similar to those attributed to Jesus, such as *The Sower*, amongst many others. The manuscripts were later brought from India to Nepal and Makhada in approx-imately AD 200, and then from Nepal to Tibet, and today are carefully preserved at Lhassa. Notovitch said that Tibetan trans-lations of the Pali text can be found in various Buddhist monas-teries, one of these being Himis. It was while Nicolas Notovitch was laid up with a broken leg in the monastery at Himis that he was actually shown the translation of the ancient scrolls. In fact, it was this experience that led him to publish his book, *Life of Jesus Christ* published in French, which also included a documented account of his travels, now published in English.

Although it is known that after the crucifixion Jesus was known by many names, he travelled incognito under the name of Yuz Asaph (Asaf). This name is also a Hebrew name. The word Yuz is another form of Yuyu, which is Jesus in the Old Persian language, or Yasu which is also Jesus in the Arabic New Testament translated from the Greek. Although there appear to be contradictions as to the interpretation of the name, the word Yuz means Jesus and Asaph is a biblical name meaning 'collector' or 'gatherer'. Jesus' sole mission was to bring all the scattered lost tribes of Israel into one fold. When he came to preach to the Lost Ten Tribes in Persia, Afghanistan and Kashmir, he was given the name Yuz Asaph — Jesus Asaph. As I have said in an earlier chapter, some writers on the subject even suggested that the tomb in Srinagar is in actual fact the tomb of Buddha. This most probably arises from all the similarities previously given between the teachings of Jesus and Buddha. Besides, the name Yuz Asaph is a Hebrew name and cannot be taken for another form of Budistava. When a detailed analysis is actually made of all the evidence and historical facts, it is quite absurd to think that the tomb in Srinagar known as the Rozabal contains the remains of Gautama Buddha, as he died in Kusinagra or Kusinara and was cremated. The tomb in Kashmir is most certainly the sepulchre of the Prophet Prince Jesus of Nazareth, who was also known as Issa and Yuz Asaph. As the Christian world knows, the fundamental doctrines of the Christian Church are primarily based upon the death of Jesus on the cross, his resurrection and bodily ascension to heaven. Even though there are eight million Christians in the world today, fewer people now accept the authenticity of these supernatural events. Nor is there any concrete evidence to sustain the theory of the death of Jesus on the cross, and even less evidence to support the phenomena of the resurrection and the ascension to heaven. Even the Gospels offer the most formidable refutations of these myths that have for so long been the very foundation of Christianity. The authentic precepts and teachings of Jesus prove nothing more than he was a prophet raised in Israel particularly for the guidance of the 'Lost Sheep of the House of Israel' (Mathew 15: 24). Jesus never claimed to be God incarnate or even the Son of God. He knew that his prayers would be answered, which is why in the Garden of Gethsemane he prayed for the cup (of death upon the cross) to be taken from him (Mathew 26: 39). Although Jesus prayed to be spared from death on the cross, it wasn't until he had actually been crucified that he began to doubt that he would be saved by God. He cried out, 'Eli, Eli, lama sabachthani', which means *My God, My God, why hast though forsaken me* (Mathew 27: 46). It is clear from this biblical narration of the event that Jesus did not expect to die, but to be delivered from the cross. This is just a further piece of evidence that Jesus did survive death by crucifixion.

Chapter Ten

Discovery of Another Tomb

In 1980 during extensive excavation work, a tomb was discovered in the Jerusalem suburb of Talpiot. The tomb contained ten limestone bone boxes (ossuaries) dated to the first century. Although the discovery of the tomb was nothing unusual in itself, six inscriptions attracted the interest of archaeologists. Corresponding to the names of Jesus, his family and some of his disciples, the inscriptions fuelled speculation that they had in fact stumbled upon the tomb of Jesus. The inscriptions were: *Jesua, son of Joseph; Mary; Mariamene e Mara; Mathew; Jofa; and Judah, son of Jesua*. Attempts have been made to prove that *Mariamene e Mara* is Mary Magdalene, and that she and Jesus had a son named 'Judah son of Jesua'. A DNA analysis concluded that tissues from the ossuaries of Jesua and Mariamene e Mara were not related, raising the possibility that they may in fact have been married and had a child. It was suggested that the statistical improbability of these names belonging to another family than that of Jesus Christ is 600 to 1. However, this suggestion has been challenged by scholars who claim that the names inscribed in the tomb were quite common at that time. Although the remains were discovered in an ancient tomb, thousands of similar tombs have been unearthed in and around the area of Jerusalem, causing many other experts to be skeptical of the find. Dr Craig Evans, PhD, author of *Jesus and the Ossuaries*, said the tomb contained the bones of about 35 different individuals, and half of these were from the same ossuaries. He also said that the site of the tomb was considerably contaminated, probably making any accurate analysis of the remains quite difficult. The other point that has been questioned by experts is the accuracy of the names. Some were written in Aramaic, others in Hebrew, and one in Greek. This would suggest that they were buried at different times. Dr Evans stated that it is not even clear that the name of 'Jesus' is actually inscribed on any of the ossuaries. The examination he made of the ossuaries was fairly inconclusive. Stephen Pfann, biblical scholar at the University of the Holy Land in Jerusalem is also unsure that the name 'Jesus' on the caskets was actually read correctly, and that it is more likely to be the name 'Hanun'. It was also suggested that Ancient Semitic script is notoriously difficult to decipher, and so speculative analysis is not a sufficient process to reach positive conclusions. Dr Evans commented that the names Jesus, Mary and Joseph were extremely common at that time, in the first century. Twenty five percent of the women during the lifetime of Jesus were named Mary. One in ten men had the name Jesua, and the name Joseph was also very popular at that time. He said that 100tombs bearing the name Jesus have been discovered in Jerusalem, and approximately 200 bearing the name Joseph, but the number of tombs bearing the name Mary is far higher. In fact, all the names inscribed in the tomb, with the one exception of Mariamene, were common to that period. It is really only because of the combination of names discovered in the tomb that speculation arose about the possibility that the remains of Jesus' family had in fact been found. However, New Testament scholar, Richard Baucham asserted that 'the names with biblical resonance are so common that even when you run the probabilities on the group, the odds of it being the famous Jesus' family are very low'.

It would then appear that the tomb's authenticity is solely dependent on whether or not the remains are really those of Mary Magdalene. Did the name Mariamene e Mara really mean Mary Magdalene? Most experts are adamant that it does not, and that Magdalene would not have been called that at her death. The assumptions made by some that the tomb is that of Jesus and his family have been totally rejected by the majority of experts on the subject for more than one reason.

In the time of Jesus it was the custom to bury the dead in their home town, and so why would Jesus' family tomb be in Jerusalem instead of Nazareth? Middle East researcher and biblical anthropologist Joe Zias commented, 'The tomb has nothing whatsoever to do with Jesus. He was known as Jesus of Nazareth, not Jesus of Jerusalem, and if the family was wealthy enough to afford a tomb, which they probably were not, it would have been in Nazareth, not in Jerusalem'. Zias completely dismissed the suggestion that the tomb was that of Jesus' family. Also, as Jesus' survival had to be kept secret, why would the family tomb be situated in Nazareth? But then again, why would it even be in Jerusalem. If this was really the tomb in which Jesus was buried, why didn't the Jewish leaders expose it? It is a known fact that the word got out that Jesus had not died on the cross, which is the very reason he travelled to India. The leaders of the synagogue searched extensively for the body of Jesus, and even accused his disciples of stealing it. The Jewish leaders despised Jesus sufficiently to want him to be crucified, and discovering his tomb, if one existed, would have been viewed as a great victory. As the Romans were in total control of Jerusalem, surely they would have been aware of the tomb. In that case why are there no written records of its existence, and why didn't contemporary Roman or Jewish historians make the tomb's whereabouts known? In fact, the Roman soldiers had been guarding the tomb to where Jesus had been taken after the cruci-fixion, and therefore knew that his body had gone missing. New Testament scholar Darrel Bock said, 'Why would Jesus' family or followers bury his bones in a family plot and then turn around and preach that he had been physically raised from the dead and had then ascended to heaven?' Furthermore, why would the disciples of Jesus allow themselves to be subjected to torture for claiming Jesus had resurrected, if they knew it was all a hoax?

Jody Magness, an archaeologist at the University of North Carolina at Chapel Hill, said that at the time of Jesus, wealthy families buried their dead in tombs cut by hand from solid rock, putting the bones in niches in the walls and then, later, transferring them to ossuaries. She went on to say, Jesus came from a poor family that, like most Jews of the time, probably buried their dead in ordinary graves. 'If Jesus' family had been wealthy enough to afford a rock-cut tomb, it would have been in Nazareth, not in Jerusalem'.

She further went on to explain the names on the Talpiot Ossuaries indicate that the tomb belonged to a family from Judea, the area around Jerusalem, where people were known by their first name and father's name. As Galileans, Jesus and his family members would have used their first name and home town. 'This whole case (for the tomb of Jesus)' she continued, 'is flawed from beginning to end'.

William G. Dever, an unbiased scholar, who has been excavating ancient sites in Israel for fifty years, and who is widely considered the dean of biblical archaeology among US scholars said, 'I am not a Christian. I am not a believer. I do not have a dog in this fight. I just think it is a shame the way the story of the tomb is being hyped and manipulated'.

Had the world leading authorities on the subject suggested that the remains in the tomb were really those of Jesus and his family, we would then have to reconsider the evidence that the Rozabal located in Srinagar, Kashmir really contains the body of Jesus. This simply proves that the story of Jesus surviving the crucifixion to live on to a good age in Kashmir is still more than a possibility as well as the greatest conspiracy of all time.

Chapter Eleven

Esoteric Christianity

As I have explained earlier, throughout antiquity, there has been evidence of a recondite knowledge that could only be given to those who were spiritually ready to receive it. This knowledge, or gnosis, contained valuable information of the things that *are*, and of the things that are yet to *be*. Although very generally known as the 'Mysteries', this secret knowledge could never be written down, and could only be passed on from teacher to pupil, 'mouth to ear'. Even then, the individual was subjected to the most arduous tests and trials, thereby proving their worthiness to receive it. The mysteries in fact revealed the truth about the origins of man, his real nature and unfolded to the initiate the secrets of supersensual worlds and beings, as well as of the natural laws of the physical world. Those who were worthy to have this knowledge entrusted to them held on to it as though it were gold. Although it has briefly been mentioned in a previous chapter, here I would like to explore the nature of the Mystery Teachings and Gnosticism a little further.

The Gnostics were an elite group responsible for the propagation of a core of teachings consisting of some elements of Christianity and other doctrines combined with their own teachings. In fact, Gnosticism was comprised of an assortment of esoteric traditions and embraced occult concepts, magic rituals and astrological predictions. In 1945, what was purported to be the Gnostic Gospels were discovered in Upper Egypt, near the town of Nag Hammadi. Written in Coptic, the ancient writings were comprised of 52 documents, in 13 leather-bound papyrus codices and were all meticulously handwritten. Containing far more information than the New Testament, the ancient writings appeared to be the authentic history of the life of Jesus and threw even more light on the so-called missing years. Although the Gnostic Gospels were a revelation, some scholars were still very skeptical about their content. They were dated about 110 to300 years after the birth of Jesus, and although every book contained in the Gnostic Gospels carried a name of a New Testament figure, (such as the Gospel of Philip, the Gospel of Peter, the Gospel of Mary, and so on) scholars dismissed the authenticity of the author's names as incorrect. In fact, one expert suggested that they were written by anonymous authors.

It is known that the early church leaders unanimously branded the Gnostics as a cult, and a secret body whose sole intention was to distort the true word of Christ. One hundred and forty years before the Council of Nicaea, Church Father Irenaeus was categorical that the Gnostics had been condemned by the church as heretics, and totally rejected their Gospels. Norman Geisler, a New Testament scholar commented, 'The Gnostic writings were most certainly not written by the apostles, but by men in the second century, and later, pretending to use apostolic authority to advance their own teachings. Today this is called fraud and forgery'. It has also been suggested that it was the intention of the Gnostics to create a false image of Jesus to further their own cause and to increase the recruitment figures for their own organization. This meant that in order to fit perfectly into their own system of thought, they needed to reinvent Jesus and make him into an omnipotent, divine non-human being. Scholars have claimed that Gnosticism is a mixture of Christian and mythical beliefs propagated by a group whose sole intention was to mystify their own name. Whilst many scholars consider that Gnosticism was originally a heretic branch of Christianity, some suggest that traces of Gnostic systems existed centuries before the Christian era, and that Gnostic sects may have possibly existed earlier than the first century BC, thus predating the actual birth of Jesus.

Although there is some suggestion that a prerequisite of Gnostic membership was the cultivation of spiritual powers, this may not have been the case with all of them. As in all walks of life, some of the members of this elite sect were in it for their own ends and to obtain power. It is said that these individuals gradually brought the elite organization into disrepute and that this was the primary reason why they were branded heretics. Some scholars suggested that Gnosticism was always considered a heretical branch of Christianity, even though as previously mentioned there is some evidence that certain Gnostic systems existed centuries before Christianity. The movement is believed to have spread in areas controlled by the Roman Empire, Arian Goths and Persian Empire. Its gradual development in the Mediterranean and Middle East before and during the second and third centuries, most probably gave rise to the skepticism about its aims and beliefs. The number of Gnostic traditions was greatly reduced in the Middle Ages with the conversion of Middle Eastern countries to Islam and the Albigensian Crusade, 1209–1229.

In the late nineteenth and twentieth century numerous esoteric and mystical traditions throughout Europe became greatly influenced by Gnosticism, and today students of occultism and similar mystical systems fully realize that the subjects they are studying originates from Gnostic teachings in one form or another.

Once all the early Christian Fathers all passed away, their successors became overzealous in their desire to transform Christianity, creating something that was certainly not there at the beginning. The true devotees of Jesus were driven underground for fear that they would be silenced by the Christian radicals, who sought only to glorify their own teachings, even if this meant misusing and prostituting the authentic Christian doctrine. As time passed by, the authentic accounts of Jesus' life became enshrouded in mystery, and the way in which his teachings were actually presented to the masses bore very little resemblance to the way they originally were. The exoteric teachings of Jesus gave the wrong impression and were built up by theologians in an edifice of dogmatic theory. The esoteric teachings became known only to a few who guarded them as though they were in possession of a valuable casket of gold.

Although the doctrines of reincarnation and karma are not a part of Christian teachings today, and are mostly viewed as being imports from India, Egypt or Persia, to the early Christian Fathers these were integral parts of Christian doctrine. In fact, the biblical narration of Jesus talking about John the Baptist (Matt.11:14) is clearly a reference to reincarnation, when he declared, 'This is Elijah that is to come'. And then he repeated, 'But I say unto you that Elijah is come already, but they knew him not, but did unto him whatsoever they would ... Then understood the disciples that he spoke unto them of John the Baptist' (Matt. 17: 12–13). This is passed over too lightly and its true meaning obviously ignored by Christians today. Moreover, the doctrines of karma and reincarnation were most certainly an integral part of the teachings Jesus propagated during his ministry. The twin-doctrines of karma and reincarnation were removed from the original teachings and completely ignored by the hierarchy of the early Church sometime around the sixth century. These were condemned as heretical teachings by the Second Council of Constantinople (AD 553), and from that time on Christianity viewed karma and reincarnation with great disdain, and saw them as an affront to God. Those who still held on to these sorts of doctrines were either driven out, imprisoned or even killed.

Little wonder then that the esoteric teachings of Christianity were discussed in secret and made known only to a chosen few. Word quickly got out that Jesus had survived the crucifixion, and although this eventually became common knowledge amongst the Christian leaders, it is was obviously in their best interests to keep the news of his survival away from the masses, and to replace it with the story of his ascension to heaven. Viewed in this way, one can see exactly why the whole story about his death was created to the way it is traditionally accepted today. At least this way Christians throughout the world would believe that he actually died on the cross to save mankind, thus making him more the archetypal deity, or as all Christians today believe, that he is the Son of God. Although very few in the Western world know that Jesus survived the crucifixion, and that his tomb is to be found in Srinagar, Kashmir, the very fact that he survived execution on the cross does not take away one single thing from the story of Jesus as a master and great teacher, but only suffices to glorify his name even more by proving, beyond a shadow of doubt, that he was a great man, and that God listened to his prayer for help and did not allow his earthly life to end on the cross.

After the supposed death of Jesus, it is known that many mystical sects and occult organizations were established all over the East. There was an awful lot of rivalry amongst them at that time, as each one claimed to be in possession of the absolute truth about the life of Jesus and the teachings he expounded. Although the majority of these gradually failed in their attempt to convince the serious devotees of the mystical doctrines, some grew in strength, and even today can still be found in certain parts of the Western world as well as in the ancient parts of the East.

Chapter Twelve

The Messianic Line

There are today innumerable theories (some quite bizarre) about the life and work of Jesus, and how he lived on for some years after the crucifixion. Collectively these different ideas have only sufficed to scratch the surface of an extremely vague and ambiguous story, and yet one that has caused sufficient intrigue amongst religious scholars and historians for it to be investigated even further. Little wonder that the life of Jesus has been an inspiration for many writers who have fully exploited the subject, distorting the story even further. One author posed the question, 'Did Jesus ever exist at all?' He even offered many valid reasons why this may have really been the case. Nonetheless, the faithful followers of Christianity persist with their belief regardless of what has been written about Jesus, the greatest prophet of all time. Needless to say, you would be forgiven for thinking that my book is just one of the many books offering yet another theory, therefore adding even more to the confusion about the greatest conspiracy of all time.

I have been interested in the subject for many years, and even as a child, I found the biblical narration of the birth and death of Jesus very difficult to accept. In June 1976, it was announced in the news that an Indian archaeologist would be visiting England with sufficient evidence to prove beyond doubt that Jesus survived the crucifixion. For some reason this visit never happened and no more was heard of the archaeologist. Although it cannot really be proved one way or the other, the Vatican are responsible for keeping evidence quiet and preventing what they really know from reaching the public domain. It has even been suggested that the Vatican is responsible for the huge cloud of scientific doubt that was cast on the authenticity of the Turin Shroud, and that the hierarchy of the Roman Catholic Church are in full possession of the facts about Jesus surviving the crucifixion. Some of the earlier scientists looking at the Turin Shroud concluded that whoever was wrapped in it released an incredible outpouring of metaphysical energy, resulting in him 'coming back to life'. Even in recent documentaries about the Turin Shroud, the fact that it appears to have been a table cloth seems to have been ignored. Nor is the fact mentioned that during earlier research the image on the Shroud appeared to have coins placed over the eyes, the dates of which corresponded with the known crucifixion of Jesus. In accordance with Messianic tradition, Jesus would have carried the tablecloth with him to be used during the breaking of the bread and the drinking of the wine ceremony. Some experts on ancient Judaic tradition have suggested that the tablecloth was always used during the burial of the teacher or master to whom it belonged, as was customary in Messianic circles.

Jesus was a Master of the highest kind, and was responsible for perpetuating the Messianic tradition by passing on the wisdom to those who had earned the right to receive it. This tradition was always performed with the breaking of the bread and the passing round of the sacred chalice. Jesus is believed to have been the last in a long line of masters of the wisdom traditions. It was Jesus' intentions to transform Judaic worship and bring the people back to the original spirit of truth as taught by Moses. Although the biblical narration of his life depicts him as a passive man of peace, he was anything but this. He was a rebel — a rebel with a very important cause. He and his followers would have achieved little if they had taken the peaceful approach. Although he most definitely preached the word of peace and love, very much like the followers of the so-called 'hippy' movement in the 1960s, it has been suggested that both he and his many supporters carried some form of weapon to protect themselves. These were very hard times and Jesus had many jealous enemies as well as followers.

Although it has earlier been suggested that the crucifixion was an integral part of a plot that he and his followers had very carefully created, primarily to attract even more attention to his name, this did not involve him actually being crucified. When Pilate asked the crowds who they wanted to be crucified, they called out Jesus' name, when in actual fact they are believed to have been calling for the demise of Jesus Barabbas, and not Jesus of Nazareth.

Even with all the many contradictions it would be quite ridiculous to even think that such a man as Jesus never existed, even though it was most probably a very common name 2000 years ago. He was undoubtedly a remarkable man, well educated and endowed with metaphysical abilities. Jesus did not develop these metaphysical abilities overnight. Far from it. As well as making a meticulous study of the ancient yogic traditions, Jesus had obviously taken great pains to cultivate his faculties for the development of Siddhis, (literally meaning 'perfect abilities' or psychic powers), and most probably devoted much of his time to meditation and the practice of asanas (yogic postures) to discipline his body, mind and spirit.

Anyone with an understanding of the disciplines adopted by a yogic master should have no problem comprehending the incredible feats performed as a result of such discipline. These may include walking on water, putting the physical body into suspended animation for a great length of time, and in some very special cases, even bringing a dead person back to life, as in the case of Lazarus. In fact, these are just some of the things attributed to Jesus in the Bible. It is clear that Jesus was an exceptional man whose powers transcended human understanding, which is probably why such a huge thing was made of his abilities in the biblical narration of his life. This is clearly why later writers interjected the story of the Virgin Birth into the

Bible, and why it was so important for Jesus' life to end with the crucifixion. These myths have been perpetuated through the ages, with the true account of Jesus' life buried beneath the fabrications created by numerous writers. Even the resurrection eventually became an integral part of Christianity, with the story of Jesus physically ascending to heaven becoming the very foundation upon which the Christian doctrine was based.

The location of the tomb of Jesus is known throughout the East, and the very fact that he survived the crucifixion to live on to a ripe old age is in fact common knowledge to all Eastern traditions. Jesus' sepulchre, known as the Rozabal, located in Srinagar, Kashmir, is the subject of pilgrimages from all over the world. Yuz Asaph is widely known throughout the East, and in fact is accepted as being Jesus, the Prophet of the People of the Book. Scholars, who know and accept the fact that Jesus survived the crucifixion to live the rest of his life in Kashmir, all agree that this does not take away anything from the beautiful story of Christianity. Nor does it make Jesus any less the man that Christians all over the world believe him to be. On the contrary, his survival of the crucifixion suffices to prove that the God Jesus worshipped was a just and compassionate god, and someone who answered his prayer to be *delivered from the hour.*

The story of Jesus as depicted in the Bible is without a doubt, the greatest conspiracy of all time, the truth of which is today being revealed to the whole Christian world. There is absolutely nothing whatsoever complicated about the story of Jesus and the fact that he lived on after the crucifixion. However, the question must be asked — is the Christian world ready for the truth?

Further Interesting Facts

Although according to the biblical narration of Jesus' childhood he is supposed to have lived for the best part of it in Nazareth, there appears to be no evidence whatsoever that such a place as Nazareth even existed during his lifetime. Nazareth is mentioned for the first time no earlier than the third century AD, and so the name 'Nazareth' has clearly been interpolated by later writers, for some reason best known to themselves. It has been suggested by some researchers of the subject that the interjection of Nazareth was some sort of a 'cover-up', a further attempt at burying the truth about Jesus even further. However, the oldest Christian site possibly in the world, is the Syro-Malankaran, whose adherents claim that St Thomas himself baptized the first of them when he landed on its coast in AD59. As the term 'Christian' had not at that time yet come into use, he referred to them as 'Nazarenes'. This merely suffices to add even more confusion as to the existence of Nazareth, unless of course the term had another connotation and did not refer in anyway whatsoever to a place called Nazareth.

Another interesting fact, which I have previously covered, is the missing years of Jesus. The majority of Christians rely on their faith and just accept the Bible's account of his life. Various religious scholars have suggested that during the years of Jesus' absence from the Bible that for two decades he may have been taken under the wing of the rabbis and priests who wanted to educate him in secret Judaic matters, and related traditions. Jesus was obviously a non-conformist Jew and was never going to be controlled or told what to do by anyone. From a very early age he was clearly aware that he had born with a mission, and that mission was to lead the Jewish people back to the spirit of truth. This was most probably the reason why he was despised so much by the majority of rabbis and temple elders, who secretly admired him and desperately wanted and needed him to be the long-awaited Messiah.

The numerous theories that Jesus travelled to many countries throughout his childhood as well as in his adult life has caused much speculation amongst religious scholars. To many it really doesn't seem plausible that he allegedly visited so many countries throughout the East; unless of course, his sole intention was for him to escape the jurisdiction of the Romans. Given that in those days the mode of travel was extremely limited, the journey must have been long and extremely very arduous and travelers most probably encountered innumerable problems en-route. One can't imagine what it was like for a healthy adult travelling long distances in those days, let alone for a young boy. Jesus allegedly travelled both as a boy and a young man to Parthia, Persia, Afghanistan, Egypt, China and even India. Then, after the crucifixion, when only in his early thirties, he visited those places yet again, eventually settling in Srinagar, Kashmir where he died. Even with all the available evidence, the majority of diehard Christians still dismiss the very suggestion that the sepulchre of Jesus can be found today in Kashmir. The Christian church appears to be afraid that if it accepts the fact that Yuz Asaph and Jesus were one and the same person, that it will then be forced to reassess the whole concept of Christianity. One writer on the subject put forward the evidence that the Messianic Jewish group — the Zealots — did flee from the control of the Romans to eventually settle in the Indian subcontinent. This much can be proved through ancient documents, which support the Zealot's exodus from the might of Roman aggression. So travelling great distances in those days was most certainly not beyond the bounds of possibility, even though the ordinary person did not have the luxury of travelling by air, car or ocean-going liner.

As children, we Christians were nurtured on the belief that the Three Wise Men were guided to the baby Jesus by a star in the heavens. The Star of Bethlehem is an integral part of Christmas and is something every Christian child can relate to. However, this is yet another myth that has been dispelled by scholars who are now quite adamant that the traditional Star of Bethlehem was more a Messianic symbol of the line of David than it was an astronomical phenomenon. It has also been suggested that the Star of Bethlehem, also known as 'the Messiah of Bethlehem', was the Messianic symbol that represented the Holy Dynasty on the bloodline of David, and the sacred symbol by which the Magi were guided directly to the baby Jesus. Some even referred to Jesus himself as 'The Star of Bethlehem', a shining Messianic light.

There has been much speculation as to whether or not Jesus married Mary Magdalene, to the extent that many writers have exploited the subject to the full. It is quite obvious why exactly the Christian Church — particularly the Church of Rome — dismiss the very idea as being preposterous, as in their eyes any such marriage would discredit Jesus' position as Messiah and world savior. Even with all the evidence, the church continues to dismiss the possibility that Jesus and Mary Magdalene did marry and have children, even though celibacy was not expected of a rabbi whose position in the synagogue required him to marry and produce children. Nowhere in the biblical account of Jesus' teachings is he seen to advocate celibacy, and although the Church ignores this fact, it is clear that Jesus was extremely fond of Mary Magdalene, to the extent that his disciples were jealous of her. In fact, Peter the apostle, and the alleged founder of the Catholic Church was most definitely married and was known to have travelled everywhere with his wife. In fact, the early Christian Church made a huge issue out of purity and the necessity for virginity and in 1139, marriage and sex became forbidden by the Christian Church, and celibacy also became a prerequisite for the priesthood. Even though celibacy played no part in the teachings of Jesus, the Christian Church still insists that it did. During Jesus' ministry, one of his greatest opponents and a leading body within Judaism were the Pharisees, who strongly advocated that it was a man's duty to marry and have children. It is quite clear that had Jesus not been married the Pharisees would have used this to criticize him further. The Christian Church appears to turn a blind eye to this fact and only accepts what suits it. Furthermore, before Paul (who was a devout bigot) became a Christian, he too was a Pharisee, and would have most certainly criticized Jesus for his celibacy. As Paul never referred to Jesus not being married, we can only assume that he clearly was.

It is clearly not in the Church's best interest to reveal to the Christian world the fact that Jesus survived the crucifixion to live on to a ripe old age in Kashmir. The church has always had a vested interest in the traditional story of Jesus and is desperate to perpetuate the myth that all Christians have grown up with, even though it is all based on falsehood. The tomb of Yuz Asaph (some call him Yus Asaf) is situated in Anzimar, Khanyar, Srinagar, known as the summer capital of Kashmir. Srinagar literally means the 'City of the Sun', and is an ancient city. Srinagar is divided into two parts — the old city and the new city, and the tomb of Yuz Asaph is located in the old city. The tomb is known locally as Rozabal, meaning 'the site of the honored tomb' and is the tomb of Yuz Asaph a prophet who settled there and who preached in the parables of Christ. The majority of the inhabitants of Srinagar refer to the tomb as the tomb of Jesus, whilst others say it is the tomb of the Prophet of the People of the Book. It is clear that the conspiracy for the Christian Church to conceal the truth about Jesus has always been apparent.

On his return to Europe sometime between 1877-1878, the writer and traveler, Nicholas Notovitch (mentioned elsewhere in the book), took his startling revelation concerning his discovery of ancient manuscripts relating to Jesus in Tibet to Monsignor Platon, the celebrated Archbishop of Kiev. Although it was Notovitch's sole intention to publish his findings, Monsignor Platon did not share his excitement and made every attempt to dissuade him from making his discovery public. The Archbishop gave Notovitch a stern warning and told him it would not be in his best interests to publish such work. Although no valid explanation was given to the writer, he decided not to pursue it any further. A year later, he took the written account of his findings to Rome and submitted his manuscript to one of the Vatican's high ranking cardinals. To Notovitch's surprise he met with a harsher and more disappointing response. He was in fact warned in no uncertain terms that if he published such a discovery he would make many enemies. He was even offered monetary compensation in return for his manuscript, which he naturally refused. Notovitch then took his manuscript to Cardinal Rotelli whom he had previously met in Constantinople, and was greatly surprised that he too opposed his work, again giving the writer a further stern warning. Cardinal Rotelli told Notovitch, 'The church suffers too deeply from this new current of atheistic ideas, and you would only furnish new food to the detractors of the Evangelical Doctrine'. Notovitch went ahead nonetheless and published his book under the title *The Unknown Life of Jesus*, and then went on to say, 'Before criticizing my work, scientific societies can without much expense, organize an expedition whose mission it would be to study these manuscripts in the locality in which they are to be found, and thus verify their historical value'. The manuscripts in question were just a small portion of the ancient documents Notovitch discovered during his sojourn in a Tibetan monastery, and which highlighted the visit of Issa to Tibet and India, confirming beyond any doubt that Jesus did preach in India to the sons of Israel. The ancient documents told of Jesus' visit when he was a young boy and then again when he was an adult, probably during his travels after the crucifixion.

Many ancient documents proving that Jesus was alive after the crucifixion are believed to lie buried in Vatican library archives. Those in charge of such important records simply choose to ignore that they even exist for fear that the truth will be revealed to the Christian world, thereby causing the Catholic Church to lose its control and bring down the greatest conspiracy of all time. There is now far too much evidence to support the fact that that Jesus did not die on the cross, and in fact went on to live a long and full life in Kashmir. Muslim scholars are also allegedly in possession of important ancient documents detailing the life of Jesus after the crucifixion. With so much evidence available one has to pose the question: Is the Christian world ready for the truth? Or maybe the majority of Christians today are content to live their lives believing that Jesus was born of a virgin and died on the cross to save us all? For many years, the Vatican has been accused of suppressing important documented evidence that Jesus not only survived the crucifixion, but that he carried on preaching for many years after, and lived on to be at least 129.

It was clear that after his crucifixion Jesus could not remain in Palestine. Some documents have suggested that with the support of close friends and the collusion of the Roman Prefect, Pontius Pilate, Jesus was spared from a long-drawn-out death on the cross. It has been further suggested that Jesus gave Pilate his word that in return for being spared that he would quietly leave Palestine. As I have previously said in the early part of this book, Jesus' survival was most definitely a political plot more than it was a religious argument. Jesus was highly intelligent and had been educated in various religious and esoteric traditions. The true nature of his teachings had been misconstrued by the less intelligent of the masses, and the assumption that he had claimed literally to be the 'Son of God' gave rise to a lot of anger. Pilate was not a stupid man and could see what Jesus was really trying to say — *the Spirit of God is in all men* and not just in Jesus. Although Pilate could not be outwardly seen to be taking the side of Jesus, at the same time he was not about to allow him to be subjected to such a horrific death. Jesus gave Pilate his word that he would leave Judea. This much is quite clear — Jesus did leave Judea with his family, Mary Magdalene, his mother Mary, Thomas and James (his brothers) and a few other close devotees. But, where did he go to first?

Even though the biblical narration suggests that a short while after the crucifixion Jesus ascended to heaven and that was that; anyone with the slightest bit of intelligence would question this and see it as a little far-fetched and fanciful. In Jesus' younger years, he had been known to have studied the Mystery Traditions in Egypt, and so it was suggested that perhaps he returned there to continue his ministry. If he did return to Egypt, which part would he have gone to? Various sources suggest that as Alexandria was dominated by the family of Philo and the Jewish Roman general Tiberius, it was highly unlikely that he would have gone there. They would not have made a Jewish Messiah very welcome, regardless of his mystical reputation, of that we can be certain. Besides, historical records show that Tiberius had persecuted and in fact slaughtered many thousands of Zealot sympathizers when they had rebelled against the Romans in Judea, and so Jesus would not have been too welcome in Alexandria. Jesus' primary concern at this time would have been for the safety of his family, and knowing of the great tension there between the Greeks and the Jews, Jesus would not have risked his family being hurt in anyway whatsoever. Although it is known that Jesus and his entourage did sojourn for a while in Egypt, where exactly is not quite clear. As I have previously said elsewhere in this book, Jesus' journey into Kashmir can be historically traced through the Valley of Yusu Margh, which is most certainly named after him. Although a great part of Jesus' travels is left to speculation, most of the places he travelled to and the things he did are well documented all over the East.

The tomb of Yuz Asaph (Jesus Christ) is built in the Jewish style of a sepulchre, with a room underground and a small window. The shrine is quite distinct from the Muslim shrines (typical in that area) which have Buddhist style conic domes. It is visited throughout the year by pilgrims and dignitaries from all over the world who come to pay homage to Yuz Asaph, the prophet of Israel. In the year of 871, Syed Nasir-ud-Din, a prophet and also a descendant of Imam Musa-Raza was buried beside Yuz Asaph. Although the sepulchre of Yuz Asaph is known to the Vatican, they simply refuse to acknowledge the fact that it may possibly contain the remains of Jesus. It was once said by a leading figure in the Catholic Church, 'We know of the tomb of Yuz Asaph in Srinagar, and the possibility that he and Jesus may be one and the same. However, to accept this publically would shake the very foundations upon which modern day Christianity is based. Therefore, such knowledge does not seem relevant when considering the deep faith and belief of devout Christians all over the world, who perceive Christianity as their extremely bright light in the darkness of a very dark and dismal world'.

Conclusion

I AM WITH THEE is an inspirational piece of prose that attempts to portray the beautiful, and yet very unusual story of Jesus and his teachings. I was inspired to write it some 25 years ago and always had an overwhelming feeling that it was the beginning of a much longer treatment of the life of the traditional Jesus.

I Am With Thee

Beneath the flickering light of a quiet room, twelve men gathered before a King, and within each saddened heart there did solemnly loom the face of an angel who sought to bring the whisper of a voice that was never to still.

And above the thrill of life that quivered unseen by the side of this man with the illumined mind, did quicken in time, the Father, the Son and the Holy Ghost, and the Spirit and the Love of All Mankind.

And the eyes that watched did look for a sign that would reveal in this man the immortal way, but the tears that fell upon the heart of the man called forth the hand that would soon betray the love of a King in an angel's gown.

The hour approached beneath a pale moon, and the shadows crept across the night, and the angels wept with solemn frown as they peered from heaven through the ephemeral light at a man who would soon betray the hand that caressed, and for a ransom, with a kiss the Sacred Heart would scorn, and in the flickering light the twelve were blessed by the man some were to deny before dawn.

The bread was as flesh, and the wine as the blood of the man before whom the twelve did pray; and as heads were bowed and voices stilled, so uttered were the words: 'In betraying me thou thyself betray. For betrayed tho' I am thy faint heart shall I not decry. For tho' my fate is at the mercy of those who would my father scorn, neither my cause nor my name shall ever die. For my Father and I are one; and together in each and every heart shall we ever reside. And betrayed tho' I shall be by those whom I love, in that love shall I always abide. For I am with thee, and so shall be even unto the end of time. Would that the hour need not dawn when my blood must spill with the blood of those who seek the sacred sign beyond all that I do not proclaim as mine. Yea, even those who blindly mock my name shall in their time my house approach. For all men shall come to me the same, and by whatsoever road they approach shall I be with them. For truly do I bear the semblance of many gods, and so must always stand as I really am in the hearts of men. But then the day shall come when I shall again arise, and so then shall call forth those who have so faithfully served my cause'.

And with this the sacred pledge was served.

And so beneath the hush of a day that lingers still in the infant heart and child unborn, did a kiss betray the love of a king to the eyes of those who would seek to scorn the ways of a man who sought only to bring thoughts divine to the faithless mind.

Alas, soon was he to find, as did those who had come before, that man shall always make impure the most sacred of men, especially those who would the Holy Word proclaim.

And so, accused before the Roman Court, with shame they did bring the man the Jews did hail as 'King' tho' others merely thought a fool.

And with cruel heart they did mock the heart of the man who wept for those men yet to come tho' even now had been denied.

And so upon the request of fools was he tried in crown of thorns and crimson gown, as all of paradise looked down in shame at those who did before the hour rejoice.

The choice was quickly made; a thief was freed, the man again betrayed, as voices called for his demise, and so the cries for mercy and angels' tears dissolved beneath the morning sky.

As the hour turned and time passed by, his feeble form was bared beneath lash and icy stare, and eager hands did then prepare for the death of a man whose name time alone would never still.

And upon a cross his back was laid, hands pierced with nails and feet with leather bound; and upon a hill the cross was raised between two men who this day their salvation found, beside the man the Jews did hail as 'KING'.

And so grey clouds unfurled across the sun, and shadows came upon the day, and angels watched as a mother wept, as she before the cross did lay at the feet of a man in whom a thousand spirits did in anger rise. It was before the eyes of those who watched did the mighty quiver and the faithless weep, and the traitor did in shadows creep, his form in twisted thread to fall lifeless from a tree beside a grey crumbling wall.

'The betrayer himself has now betrayed!' the angels did cry, 'So shall it be with all those who deny the man who gave his life that he might in thy hearts forever live'.

The warning had been called; a hush befell the hour; the end had come so to devour the body of a man but not the soul.

And so in the Holy Tomb secure in linen bound did he so lie, as in the garden light obscure did curious eyes seek to pry upon those who did in shadows mourn.

The night passed by, and so the day did gently dawn, dissolving shadows and nightly gloom, so revealing through the filtered light the empty, solemn tomb of a King to the eyes of those who did in their vigilance abide.

'The Lord has risen!' A man cried and a woman did weep, and so the secret that time had sought to keep was brought to the ears and the hearts of men. But then it was in the garden when the air was still, and sweet perfumes did fill the night, and everything was lost in an ocean of dreams and shimmered beneath the pale moonlight, did he to the faithful once more appear; so to fulfill a promise to those who cared, and his sweet memory in their loyal hearts to endear.

'My work is done!' said he, 'Through death shall my soul to heaven rise, beyond the cries of the faithless and those who did my Sacred Heart scorn; but so too shall man in darkness die, tho' into light shall his soul be born. For death alone shall not devour the man in whom I do dwell. And I shall tell you once again: I am with thee, and so shall be even unto the end of time. Yea, even those who blindly mock my name shall in their

time my house approach. For all men shall come to me the same, and by whatsoever road they approach shall I be with them. For truly do I bear the semblance of many gods, and so must always stand as I really am in the hearts of men. But then, the day shall come when I shall again arise, and so shall call forth those who have so faithfully served my cause'.

The story is not yet complete...

AXIS MUNDI
BOOKS

Axis Mundi Books provide the most revealing and coherent explorations and investigations of the world of hidden or forbidden knowledge. Take a fascinating journey into the realm of Esoteric Mysteries, Magic, Mysticism, Angels, Cosmology, Alchemy, Gnosticism, Theosophy, Kabbalah, Secret Societies and Religions, Symbolism, Quantum Theory, Apocalyptic Mythology, Holy Grail and Alternative Views of Mainstream Religion.